Looking at Inclusion

Listening to the voices of young people

Ruth MacConville
Stephen Dedridge
Ann Gyulai
Janet Palmer
Lisa Rhys-Davies

P·C·P

Paul Chapman
Publishing

Paul Chapman Publishing
A SAGE Publications Company
1 Oliver's Yard
55 City Road
London EC1Y 1SP

SAGE Publications Inc.
2455 Teller Road
Thousand Oaks, California 91320

SAGE Publications India Pvt Ltd
B 1/I 1 Mohan Cooperative Industrial Area
Mathura Road, Post Bag 7
New Delhi 110 044

SAGE Publications Asia-Pacific Pte Ltd
33 Pekin Street #02-01
Far East Square
Singapore 048763

www.luckyduck.co.uk

Library of Congress Control Number: 2006904040

British Library Cataloguing in Publication data

A catalogue record for this book is available from the British Library

ISBN 978-1-4129-1911-1

Typeset by C&M Digitals (P) Ltd, Chennai, India
Printed in Great Britain by the Cromwell Press, Trowbridge, Wiltshire
Printed on paper from sustainable resources

Looking at Inclusion

A Lucky Duck Book

This book is dedicated to the children and young people in the London Borough of Ealing

Contents

Acknowledgements

This book has grown from the enthusiasm and partnerships of practitioners, young people and their families, working together as a co-operative team. Together we have shared the growth and development of our thoughts and ideas to produce *Looking at Inclusion: Listening to the Voices of Young People*. We hope that this book will be helpful for those who want to develop services that are responsive to the experiences and aspirations of young people.

First, we would like to thank the children and young people who have contributed to and lived out the ideas contained in this book and been our inspiration in writing it. Also thank you to the head teachers, staff and parents in Ealing's schools. Without their collaboration and support this book would not be possible.

The authors would also like to thank Councillor Ian Gibb, Deputy Leader of the Council and Portfolio Holder for Children and Young People, Leonora Thompson, previous Leader of the Council; and Sonika Nirwal, for their support for the Powerful Voices conferences which have informed our thinking and provided the important foundations for this book.

Thank you also to David Archibald, Executive Director for Individuals; Judith Finlay, Director of Children and Families and Hilda McCafferty, the previous director of Access and Inclusion who have also supported the Powerful Voices conferences. Special thanks also to Hilda who encouraged the production of this book from its inception. Thanks also to our colleagues and friends, especially Bridie McDonagh, Vina Mistry, Michael O'Grady, Marilyn Dedridge, James Haftel, Philip Masters, Ben Andersen, Dr Ossie Stuart and Giles Barrow, who have helped us with the development of our thinking and provided ongoing encouragement throughout the entire process of writing this book.

Finally, thanks go to our publishers, Sage Publications, and to George Robinson at Lucky Duck who has always been available for helpful advice and provided invaluable encouragement throughout.

Dr Ruth MacConville
Stephen Dedridge
Ann Gyulai
Janet Palmer
Lisa Rhys-Davies

Foreword

Over the last ten years we have heard much that has been written using the language of empowerment. We have been regaled with words and phrases which have sought to emphasise the central role of children and young people in the decisions taken regarding their educational and social lives: voice, opportunity, listening ... and so on. While used undoubtedly with honesty and meaning, there is a view, frequently expressed, that such language has been hijacked by politicians, educational opportunists and ideologues. This has resulted in cynicism towards these terms, and their grudging acceptance as yet another checklist or policy which needs to be 'done'. The phrase 'lip-service' springs to mind.

As evidence of this one has simply to turn to the array of checklists, proformas and indices which seek to assess the extent of inclusion in schools and settings. All emphasise the importance of listening to children, yet few offer much evidence that any real listening to children or young people has taken place.

So it is refreshing when one can be reminded of the frequent examples where there is genuine, embedded, but nevertheless routine, involvement of children in their own learning. *Looking at Inclusion: Listening to the Voices of Young People* provides a case in point. It urges – even commands – us to pay rigorous attention to the accounts that children and young people (what an anaemic and managerialist term 'stakeholder' is!) give of their experiences in schools and other settings. Listening and hearing, it suggests, are of little account unless there is resultant action.

The contributors of this book have, no doubt, been corralled, press-ganged or blackmailed into providing personal accounts of their work. Most practitioners that I encounter, professionals who have commitment, expertise and creativity and use it to enhance the education of a significant population of children and young people, are diffident about 'publicising' their work. For them the doing of it is by far more important than reporting it to a wider audience. So the lead author of the volume must have exercised considerable powers of persuasion to secure her colleagues' contribution.

The product is a wonderfully textured, varied and real-life account of how we can enable children and young people to participate in important decisions that are made relating to their own education. There is little space here to explore in detail the varied and intricate range of examples of inclusionary practice offered in this book. Suffice it to say that you will find a collection of materials which offer us hope that we are moving perceptibly away from the opportunistic use of the terms of empowerment. These chapters offer hope that – to use another adage – actions speak louder than words. We should feel grateful that these writers have dispelled any diffidence and reserve, in order to communicate their experiences to us.

Professor Philip Garner
University of Northampton

Introduction

This book is about emphasising the voices of pupils with disabilities and listening to what they have to tell us about themselves. What does it mean to be a pupil with a disability who is included in a mainstream school? What perceptions and experiences do pupils with disabilities have and what do they say about themselves, their identities, their relationships and their perceptions of their fit with their mainstream environment? If we seriously want to know the answers to these questions, we need to make time and listen. We need to enable pupils to talk to us about themselves in their own words and without the restrictions of others. This book represents a vehicle for the pupils' voices as they tell us about their lives. We believe that it is important that readers know what pupils have to say. This book also provides an opportunity for us to emphasise the resilience and strengths that the pupils possess; the fact that for the most part pupils with disabilities are 'actively seeking inclusion' (Allan, 1999).

The purpose of this book, then, is to convey to readers what pupils with disabilities have told us about their experience of school and of being included. The authors are teachers and members of a support service working within a recently formed Children's Service in the London Borough of Ealing and this book reflects our work with pupils, schools and families. The methods that we used to collect the pupils' observations and perspectives did not follow a strict methodology. As a team we agreed with Hart's (1996) observation that 'the knowledge and skills which a teacher has already acquired through teaching can be sufficient in themselves for generating new knowledge and understanding without necessarily needing to be underpinned by research design and data collection' (p. 124). Nias (1991) emphasised in relation to the validity of research that the deeper the involvement, the longer the association, the stronger the promise of groundedness. We had, before the inquiry began, already achieved persistent and prolonged professional involvement with the pupils whose views and perspectives are contained in this book.

We were aware when we embarked upon this inquiry that children and young people may be more inclined to present themselves as unrealistically competent and accepted when talking to a person who has no knowledge of their true competence and acceptance. We therefore believed that working with familiar adults reduced the potential problem of pupils' responding judiciously in a socially desirable way. While acknowledging the potential difficulties of carrying out an inquiry in familiar territory we nonetheless believed that the advantages far outweighed the drawbacks.

Emancipatory research

A primary consideration from the outset was to ensure that the inquiry was emancipatory. Emancipatory research is about putting something back, not simply carrying out an inquiry for the sake of research. We were mindful of Moore's (Moore *et al.,* 1998) observation that as soon as the decision to focus on children with disabilities is made, there is a risk of pathologising them which may lead to them being over-researched and their mainstream peers assuming the status of a normative group. An emancipatory approach entails engaging with several key issues which include establishing relationships with those with disabilities, listening to their voices and asking how the knowledge and skills which emanate from the inquiry can be employed to improve their situation. For the pupils it is important that this book accurately represents the issues that they have told us are important. We also hope that this book offers our readers unique insights into the perspectives of pupils with disabilities and practical suggestions for the classroom.

The approach throughout this text has been to match the pupils' voices to existing literature and published research in the area of inclusion. We have chosen this approach in order to accentuate the realities of inclusion that pupils themselves present and also in order to respect and celebrate the autonomous pupil voice. The recognition of the power of pupil perceptions in providing alternative views of inclusion to those of practitioners is gradually increasing. Teachers have been at the forefront of the developments which enable pupils' views to be heard (MacConville, 2006a). Despite the rhetoric of the importance of the pupil voice there is a paucity of evidence about what pupils themselves think about inclusion (Gersch, 2000; Thomas *et al.,* 1998). This book seeks to address this gap. We agree with Corbett (2002) that the time has come to seek the views of pupils themselves and ask them how well school and specialist services meet their needs and how included they feel within their school.

The chapters in this book relate to the five disabilities which are represented by domains of responsibilities within the team. These are autism spectrum disorder (ASD), visual impairment, specific learning difficulties (SpLD), hearing impairment and physical disabilities. We address the learning challenges posed by disabilities and also the social challenges because during our conversations these were the issues that pupils emphasised. Although from a practitioner's point of view the ability to get on with one's peers and make friends may seem to have only a peripheral value, from the pupils' viewpoint friendships are vital. Ask a pupil about school and the response is not likely to be whether or not the curriculum is developmentally appropriate; most pupils emphasise the quality of their relationships with their peers.

Hierarchy of needs

When Maslow (1968) elaborated his hierarchy of human needs he divided them into distinct levels. Maslow saw progression from one level to another as being possible only when one's needs had been met at a lower level. This is neatly summarised in the old adage 'you cannot teach a hungry child'. Throughout the inquiry pupils emphasised their social 'belongingness' and their self-esteem needs. It is only when these needs have been met that individuals can achieve increasing autonomy. Sharp (2001) has drawn a parallel between Maslow's (1968) hierarchy and the development of emotional literacy. Sharp writes that when individuals have had their safety needs met they can move on to self-actualisation and only then will individuals achieve 'high levels of emotional literacy' (p. 14).

The central thesis of this book is that when including pupils with disabilities one needs to recognise the real nature of the task. It is about understanding disabilities at a psychological as well as at a behavioural level. Problems of shyness or lack of assertion in pupils with disabilities are endemic in schools but these problems do not always attract the same attention as those of overt behaviour difficulties yet they may be just as damaging to the individual's social and emotional development and the learning process. Our aim is to provide practitioners with the information and practical strategies that are needed in order to effectively include pupils with disabilities and enable them to move forward in their social and emotional development.

All the young people we spoke to had important and valuable contributions to make and wished their comments to be included in this book. We have only been able to include a small proportion. The contributions that we have included were chosen because they were representative; one voice speaks for many. The pupils who contributed to this book were inspired by the belief that their views matter; their honesty, commitment and courage shines through. Our warmest appreciation is reserved for them; they taught us how to listen and helped us to see what is possible.

Finally, throughout this book the authors have changed the names and all other descriptors that may identify pupils, practitioners or schools.

Dr Ruth M. MacConville

Chapter 1

Setting the Scene

Dr Ruth M. MacConville

This chapter describes the 'framework for thinking' that underpins our work and the approach which we have developed in order to engage with pupils about the issues that are important to them. The ability to 'read' pupils' behaviour and to communicate with them is captured in the analogy of being able to 'dance with the children' which implies harmony, recognising the 'steps' children are taking, being able to anticipate their next move and adapting one's response accordingly (Trevarthen, 1992). Listening to pupils' perspectives is a skilful task for which a knowledge of child development is an important prerequisite. As a team we have been inspired by the work of Giles Barrow (Barrow et al., 2001; Barrow and Newton, 2004) who introduced us to the cycles of development – a framework of thinking that is linked to self-esteem and one in which the importance of getting children's social and emotional development off to the right start is emphasised.

The cycle of development was originated by Pamela Levin (1982). Its educational potential was developed by Jean Illsley Clarke who adapted the model for parent educators (Clarke and Dawson, 1998). It was then tailored by Giles Barrow (Barrow et al., 2001) to make it suitable for school use. In collaboration with Giles we have finely tuned the model to support our work with pupils with disabilities. The approach is therefore well researched with a strong theoretical base which is relevant to classroom practice. The key to the success of the cycle of development is that it offers practitioners a systemic, flexible and proactive way of responding to a diversity of social and emotional needs. This is important because it is now widely recognised that 'effective inclusion' relies on more than specialist skills and resources; it requires positive attitudes towards children who have difficulties in school, a greater responsiveness to individual needs and, critically, a willingness among all staff to play their part (DfES, 2004: 2.7). The purpose of this chapter is to share with readers this dynamic 'thinking framework' which underpins our work.

Emotional literacy

The work of Lawrence (1996) emphasises that children who have appropriate levels of self-esteem and who feel confident about themselves achieve higher academic results and have fewer behavioural problems than pupils with low self-esteem. It is now generally recognised that being emotionally literate is as important for learning as teaching (Goleman, 1996). We are aware that learning does not take place in isolation from pupils' feelings and will only take place if a child is secure and happy. The dilemma for staff is often how to teach and at the same time successfully manage the emotional territory of the classroom. This has been exacerbated by an increasing pressure upon schools to emphasise academic instruction and the formal testing of its effects. If practitioners do not have time to think about their pupils as individuals, then pupils may not learn how to reflect upon their emotions or discover how their feelings can affect their behaviour. This is true for all pupils but has a particular significance for pupils with disabilities who are the focus of this book.

The cycle of development

The cycle of development (Clarke and Dawson, 1998) provides a robust framework for identifying significant stages in a child's social and emotional development and offers practical help for staff by emphasising timely and positive interventions. The cycle can be summarised as the process that occurs when we enter a new situation and as we gradually become familiar with that environment. In addition, therefore, to using the cycle to describe a child's emotional development from birth we can also apply the model to the process of embarking on any 'new' situations such as a child starting a new school, or an individual starting a new job or even a new relationship. As we enter a new situation there may be an initial sense of confusion and we may become passive as we begin to understand what it means to *be* in this new place. Just like a new baby we need to be welcomed and encouraged to feel we belong. As we become more familiar with a new place we begin to explore our new surroundings. Barrow and Newton (2004) emphasise that this *doing* stage is about how we feel. At this stage we need to have the opportunity to explore safely while somebody keeps watch over us. Next is the *thinking* stage when we begin to recognise the need to do things differently in the new place but don't quite know how to. Encouragement for our own thinking will enable us to take steps towards finding our new *identity*, accepting the new environment and our place in it and so enable us to move on to develop the *skills* and competences we need. For the purposes of our work with schools the critical stages in the cycle include: becoming, being, doing, thinking, identity and power, skills and structure.

Stages not ages

The work of Piaget also demonstrates that childhood development proceeds through a series of stages, giving rise to the adage 'stages not ages'. By the time they reach school age, children have an unconscious view of themselves which manifests through levels of self-esteem. In order to achieve a level of emotional literacy appropriate to their age and development children may need support to make up or compensate for components of emotional and social development that they have missed out on. The cycle of development is both dynamic and optimistic because it enables stages of development that have not been previously fully completed to be identified and revisited. The model has two important aspects for each stage of development in the child. These are developmental tasks and affirmations.

First, there are 'tasks' to be completed that are appropriate to each stage and provide the grounding on which following stages will build. In order to fully complete the developmental tasks, the child needs affirmations. Affirmations are the messages that we need to hear and learn to give at each stage of growth. Affirming encourages self-esteem. There are specific affirmations that we need to hear at each stage of growth. If a child does not receive the appropriate affirmations either from the main carers or from other people, there is likely to be a deficit in emotional growth which may hinder progress in the next and subsequent stages.

Cyclical development

In this model development is cyclical not linear. This means that we can revisit earlier stages and find what we need and missed when going through that stage the first time round. Levin (1982) emphasises that our development does not stop at the end of adolescence but continues to recycle the stages throughout our lives. For adults it offers the possibility to 'repair' gaps in development that may have caused difficulties as we recycle in a natural process. In our work with schools we have used the cycle of development in two ways. We have used it preventatively because recognising and attending to what children need at each stage promotes thriving and healthy emotional and social development. We have also used the framework restoratively. Early intervention in our work with children with disabilities is advantageous; however, for a variety of reasons this work with families sometimes does not take place. The cycle of development emphasises that it is never too late to address gaps in a pupil's emotional development and the model enables critical 'repair work' to be done. Through observation and assessment of behaviours and by ensuring children and young people receive relevant affirmations we can encourage pupils to do the developmental tasks of earlier stages that they may have missed or not fully completed. We have discovered through using this model that pupils are enabled to grow in confidence and self-esteem and create their own security, encouragement, problem-solving skills, co-operation with others, enjoyment and spontaneity.

Stages of the cycle of development

The remainder of this chapter will explore in more detail the stages of development which, in our experience, have the most significance for the inclusion of pupils with disabilities in the context of our work with schools.

Becoming

The preparatory stage of the cycle of development is 'becoming'. Just as parents prepare carefully for the birth of a child so a school at this stage also prepares for the new arrival. The knowledge that pupils with disability are going to be admitted is often a cause of concern for staff and especially for the head teacher, Special Educational Needs Co-ordinator (SENCO) or inclusion manager. Just as parents do the important work of preparing themselves, their family and friends to welcome their baby so schools also need to prepare themselves to welcome the pupil. Parents' concerns about their child starting a new nursery or school usually focus around worries that staff will not understand the trigger points of distress or respond positively to their child's communicative behaviour. In many schools work at this stage takes the form of transition projects, e.g. inviting pupils to visit the secondary school and become familiar with the new environment during the final term of primary school. Schools may also need to prepare the physical environment to ensure it is accessible. This work may include the purchase of specialist equipment, decision making around staffing, i.e. working out whether a member of staff will need to have specific responsibility for the pupil and who that person will be. Sometimes there is also the critical decision of which class the 'new' pupil will belong to. At this preparatory stage just as parents hopefully receive advice and care from those around them so schools may also seek help. Supporting schools in the process of preparing to admit a pupil with disability is an important aspect of our work. Pupils with disabilities need staff that understand their needs and have sufficient knowledge to feel confident in providing for them. Training is offered to settings before a pupil is admitted and schools are encouraged to involve as many of the school staff as possible, including midday supervisors and administrative staff who will have dealings with the pupil and should understand their difficulties. Staff may also need help and advice on producing specific resources.

Affirmations for becoming

Affirmations for the 'becoming' stage include 'Your needs and safety are important to me', 'I accept you just as you are'. These affirmations need to be appropriately translated to all 'becoming' situations. At this stage schools need to reassure parents that the needs and safety of their child are important to them and that the child will belong. Unfortunately, the 'becoming' stage can be fraught with difficulty and just as mothers may experience emotional, medical or financial concerns so schools may also be overwhelmed by a sense of their impending responsibility for a pupil with a disability. This is often expressed as concern about a scarcity of resources both in terms of finance and in terms of specialist expertise. Just as a baby born into a family where there is a sense of ambivalence about the birth is likely to have difficulties bonding, which may later negatively impact on the child's emotional and social development, so pupils with disabilities may be also adversely affected by any conflict or negativity which is associated with their admission to the school. Although of course it is crucial that schools express their needs for resources and expertise this communication should not contaminate the pupil's entry to school as it can undermine the success of the placement and the pupil's confidence and self-esteem. In Chapter 6 a pupil with a physical disability powerfully describes the negative impact his parents' struggle with the local primary school had on him.

Being

At this (birth to six months) stage in the cycle of development, the baby's important task is to decide to live and to be in the world; to accept care and touch and decide to thrive; to trust and to call out to have their needs met. These are crucial decisions which will nourish us and amplify throughout our whole lives. When babies receive love and care, are handled appropriately and when their needs are met consistently they will develop a trusting and responsive attitude which is the basic block for thriving. The baby therefore has permission 'to be', to trust, to belong, and be part of the family and community. The affirmations that the baby needs to hear at the 'being' stage are 'You belong here', 'What you need is important to me', 'I'm glad you are you', and 'You can grow at your own pace'. When the baby does not take in permission 'to be' and does not 'hear' positive affirmations associated with *being*, the results can be painful. Lillian Katz (2005) emphasises that 'parents and educators might also keep in mind what builders know only too well: if the foundations of a building are not properly laid at the outset, it can be difficult and expensive to repair later on; indeed some kinds of early errors may even be the cause of significant injuries in the future' (p. viii). The *'being'* stage is usually critical for children with disabilities because it is often in these early days that a diagnosis of disability is made. A diagnosis can have significant impact on parents' ability to bond with their child which can in turn not only undermine the child's emotional development but also render the child vunerable in entering 'new' situations in the future. There is, as a result, usually unanimous agreement within services that a key task is to work with parents in the pre-school stage and that the work should commence as soon as possible after the child's disability has been diagnosed (MacConville, 1989). In Chapter 5, the implications of the diagnosis of deafness is explored in terms of the adverse effect it can have upon the parent/child relationship.

Affirmations for being

It is essential, therefore, that pupils with disabilities 'hear' positive affirmations associated with belonging to the school and a major task for team members is to emphasise to schools the importance of building positive relationships with individual pupils and their parents right from the start. At this 'being' stage just as babies need others to be reliable and trustworthy, to provide consistent care and to affirm the baby for doing appropriate developmental tasks, so a pupil entering a 'new' nursery, primary or secondary school needs similar helpful adult behaviours and positive affirmations from a key person who has prime responsibility for establishing a relationship with the pupil and that both parents and pupil are aware of this. A pupil who does not receive 'emotional holding' (Greenhalg, 1994) during this period of entry may find it hard to trust people or to belong and therefore is likely to appear passive and uncertain in school and unable to enter the next 'doing' stage of the cycle.

Doing

At the doing or exploring stage, between the age of 6 and 18 months, the child decides to trust others and that the environment is a safe and exciting place to explore. The baby may also decide to be active and to get support while doing all these things. The child's developmental tasks at this stage are to explore and experience the environment, to signal needs and to trust others and self, to get help in times of distress, and to start to learn that there are options and that not all problems are easily solved. Pupils also need to do this 'work' in a new school. They may do this by very tentatively moving away from their key person in order to build relationships with others and begin to develop their initiative and independence as school becomes an increasingly familiar place.

Affirmations for doing

Helpful affirmations for this stage include 'I like to watch you initiate and grow', 'You can know what you know', and 'You can do as many things as you need to'. Many pupils with disabilities need a great deal of encouragement to build new relationships and begin to explore a new school environment and may often hide their needs for fear of rejection. In our experience pupils with disabilities can be fearful of the playground and usually seek a quiet and well-supervised place to spend their breaktimes. Pupils tell us that the informal and unstructured times of the school day such as breaktimes and lunchtimes can be the most challenging. When staff observe that pupils with disabilities are reluctant to move away from a key adult and seek to remain anonymous in school, the helpful response is to recognise that the pupil may continue to need that close and supportive relationship and the encouragement of that key adult in moving on. The pupil may also benefit from hearing the affirmations for 'being'. A pupil's reluctance to use what Allan (1999, p. 57) refers to as 'a marker of a disabilty' (hearing aids, glasses) at this stage is likely to be about not feeling safe enough to be different and wanting to hide away.

The peer group

A significant aspect of pupils' exploration of a new school environment is the peer group. Allan (1999, p. 111) suggests that 'pupils are the gate keepers who can by their attitude or behaviour include or exclude pupils with disabilities'. Pupils are all too aware of those individuals who stand out as being different and this attitude becomes more emphasised as pupils get older (Thompson et al., 2001). Pupils are keen to explore differences in their peers and will frequently directly confront the pupils with disabilities about differences in appearance, hearing aids or wheelchairs. The reality is that children are usually not politically correct and like straightforward answers to their questions (MacConville, 2006b). In Chapter 3 pupils with visual disabilities describe their experiences of being questioned about their disability by their peers. Pupils who have not fully completed earlier developmental tasks may not be confident enough to deal with this questioning and may seek to disguise their disability either by refusing to wear hearing aids or glasses or by simply avoiding contact with their peers. Proximity is an important antecedent of the ability to get along easily with others and therefore throughout this book the importance of supporting schools in the process of building peer support groups in order to enable pupils with disabilities to develop their ability to make friends is emphasised (MacConville and Rae, 2006).

Time to listen

Schools, of course, are notoriously busy places where a diverse range of activities, planned and unplanned, take place for pupils and staff. It is quite possible in a busy school for pupils to avoid meaningful contact if they are determined to do so. The huge pressures mean that in reality staff often do not have the opportunity to work with individual pupils unless this is specifically emphasised as part of their role. Strategic planning for pupils with disabilities means that they are increasingly taught in groups (Gross and White, 2003).

For pupils with disabilities the opportunities for building relationships with members of staff that are offered within the curriculum are frequently not enough. An important task for members of a support service is to emphasise to schools a pupil's need to develop a positive relationship with a member of staff. Staff also frequently need to be reassured that communicating with pupils with disabilities is usually not a specialist skill and should be part of the basic repertoire of everyone who works with them. The critical things that practitioners can do to enable pupils to be involved in a dialogue include: actively looking for a pupil's competence, not assuming their incompetence; using ways of communicating that pupils find helpful and giving pupils time to express their views in their own way. Taking the time to listen and encouraging pupils to express their own thoughts and feelings can give them a feeling of being more in control and enable pupils to move on successfully in terms of their social and emotional development.

Thinking

At this next stage children between the age of 18 months to 3 years begin to talk and view themselves as separate people with their own thinking. This is the stage of the 'terrible twos' and is characterised by struggle, conflict and frustration. Children at this stage typically want to do things for themselves and have powerful reactions to new experiences. The developmental tasks at this stage are for the child to learn to think, solve problems and express feelings. Typically, in terms of their experience of school, a children with a disability will at the 'thinking' stage begin to express sadness, resentment and a feeling of 'why me?' in relation to their disability. It is important for staff to accept these feelings as a necessary and positive stage in the pupil's development and as evidence, first, that the pupil feels safe enough to express sadness and frustration and, secondly, that such expressions are evidence that critical work is being accomplished.

Affirmations for thinking

Helpful affirmations for this stage will include 'You can know what you need and ask for help', 'I am glad you are starting to think for yourself', 'It's OK for you to be angry' and 'I won't let you hurt yourself and others'. Unhelpful adult behaviours towards pupils at the 'thinking' stage include discounting what the pupil is saying. We recognise that this sometimes happens because staff find it painful to address the pupil's disability. Children who do not reach this stage of beginning to think for themselves typically appear angry and disaffected in school and are likely to engage in sullen, withdrawn, rebellious behaviours.

Support groups

In partnership with school staff our response to pupils with disabilities who are at the 'thinking' stage of their development is often to establish support groups for pupils with the same disability. Such groups, which usually comprise up to eight pupils, can provide a safe mechanism for pupils to express powerful feelings about coming to terms with their disability and can also encourage joint problem-solving. During the operation of such groups we have discovered that pupils may be unaware of the significance of their disability. A pupil with Asperger's syndrome, for example, shared with 'his' group his fear that they would not live to adulthood. It transpired that this pupil's reasoning was based on the fact that he had never met an adult with Asperger's syndrome and had therefore wrongly concluded that they were suffering from a terminal condition. Deaf children of hearing parents often tell us that they will be glad when they grow out of wearing their hearing aids. Deaf pupils who have not come across a deaf adult wearing a hearing aid may assume that they will simply grow out of their deafness.

It is well-documented that parents are frequently reluctant to discuss their child's disability with their child (Corker, 1994). There is an extensive literature on the process of families' adaptation to the diagnosis of a disability and as practitioners we are frequently witness to the struggles encountered by many families in arriving at a positive view of their child and becoming confident about the best way forward. A medical condition or disability will frequently have long-term and significant implications for a family and the child may have to adapt to a different future and often the prospect of deterioration. A support group is often the first opportunity for pupils to problem-solve their future with others.

Something to say

Support groups also provide an opportunity for pupils to think about the terminology associated with their disability and how to describe it to others – what words to use. Chapter 5 describes the positive outcomes of support groups for pupils with hearing impairment.

Identity and power

Between the ages of three and six years, the child focuses on learning and activities and establishes an individual identity. By the age of three years children have usually made important decisions about themselves and how they relate to others. During this stage they will elaborate on these decisions by asking fundamental questions such as 'Who am I?', 'What's going on here?', 'What will I do tomorrow? and 'What will I do when I grow up?' Important developmental tasks for children at this stage are to become a separate person with an individual identity, to find out the results of behaviour including testing their power and to begin to learn to separate fantasy from reality.

Affirmations for identity and power

Affirmations for individuals at this stage of development include 'You can try out different roles and ways of being powerful' and 'You can learn the results of your behaviour'. Pupils who have successfully moved through the 'thinking' stage are well on the way to achieving a new identity, discovering the effect they have on others, achieving a 'new' identity and securing a place in the social landscape of the school. Chapter 5 describes a pupil who is proud to announce her deafness by wearing bright yellow hearing aids. Individuals who have accomplished a robust and individual identity are then able to develop the skills and competences that enable them to fully manage their own disability. Chapter 3 describes a pupil with a visual disability who has overcome his reluctance to use his magnifier so that he can access text messages from his peers.

Conclusion

The cycle of development has provided us with a flexible, systemic 'broad brush' approach to understanding the social and emotional needs of pupils with disabilities and a practical way of meeting their needs. We know that we have successfully shared this 'thinking framework' with schools when we recognise their emphasis on carefully preparing for and welcoming pupils with disabilities into their community and ensure that they initially allocate a key member of staff to that child and gradually from that secure relationship encourage the pupil to explore and build other relationships. We also detect the 'thinking framework' in operation when we observe staff reacting sensitively to pupils' reluctance to use 'markers of their disability' and making time to listen. The strength of the cycle of development is that it can be part and parcel of what goes on every day within the classroom, in the playground, dinner hall and corridors. Encouraging pupils to revisit and complete earlier developmental tasks and providing specific affirmations in our experience enables pupils to move successfully on in their social and emotional development. Hard evidence for the impact of the cycle of development in the form presented in this chapter is lacking at the time of writing; however, as Gross and White (2003) emphasise: 'Nor are named programmes and schemes ... necessarily more likely to succeed than some of the tailor-made approaches devised by teachers with a high degree of training and expertise for the individual children they work with' (p. 98). The cycle of development has provided us with an approach to pupil involvement which is responsive to the pupils' needs: participatory, reflexive and adaptable. It has most of all provided us with new ways of listening to children and young people whose voices will be heard in the ensuing chapters of this book.

Chapter 2

Including Pupils with Autistic Spectrum Disorder

Stephen Dedridge

Introduction

Autistic spectrum disorder (ASD) is a life-long developmental disability that affects the way the brain makes use of the information it receives. It results in the individual having a perception of the world which is different from that shared by the majority of people.

Many people with ASD experience unusual or extreme reactions to the sights, sounds and tactile sensations within their immediate environment. They also have difficulties in working out what is happening around them and in particular find the complex and ever changing world of social interaction extremely challenging.

Some people with ASD develop speech and can perform many everyday tasks independently. Their overall cognitive ability may be within the 'normal' range. Such people are sometimes referred to as 'High Functioning'. In some cases a person may be diagnosed with Asperger's syndrome which is a specific type of High Functioning ASD.

High Functioning ASD is sometimes referred to as 'mild' autism but this can be misleading as many individuals can still experience considerable difficulties in their ability to function in everyday life. This is highlighted in the following personal account, written by a teacher who has recently been diagnosed with the condition.

Personal account

Imagine, if you can, that you find it so scary to look at people's faces, especially when you are talking to them, that it becomes something you don't do very often. Imagine that you can only manage to make very brief eye contact with another person. But even if you do look at somebody's face, it is a complete mystery to you what that person is saying to you with their eyes. Facial expressions and tone of voice have to be very obvious, disturbingly dramatic even, in order for you to understand what they mean. Imagine also that you are not aware of other people's body language, much less are you able to 'read' it and intuitively understand what it means.

In these circumstances, the spoken word becomes all important because it is mostly all I have to go on and it is so hard for me to tell whether other people are being genuine. I have little means of knowing whether their body language, eye contact, etc. is consistent with the words they are speaking. I often make negative assumptions about what people think of me, or about how I might be affecting them. These assumptions are based both on past unfortunate experiences that I have had with people, and on my own somewhat negative self-image; they have very little, if anything, to do with the signals that the other person is really giving out.

An uneasy relationship

Other people have been a problem for me as long as I can remember. The way that I perceive other people, and especially the way that I feel about myself in relation to them, has always been such a huge issue for me. My relationship with other people per se has always been a distinctly uneasy and uncomfortable one.

Fear of people

The big world outside of myself is a scary place for me and I fear other people trying to take control of my environment. Other people seem quite alien to me, very different to identify with and to understand. I have never felt like one of them.

Being different

I have known since I first entered into the social world that I was different. I have always felt that I just wasn't normal but didn't know why I had such difficulty fitting in, forming relationships and coping with things such as socialising, which seemed to come so naturally and so effortlessly to everyone else. At school, I did not understand why lessons were such a frightening, confusing and humiliating experience for me.

As a teenager and as an adult, I have put considerable effort and energy into avoiding people. The fact of my being very out of touch with other people, coupled with not having a good understanding of the social rules, means that I have a very poor perception of other people's boundaries and very often do not realise the limits beyond which normal people will not go with me. This makes the world and the people in it seem terrifying, especially when I feel that I have wronged somebody, or otherwise upset them.

Self-esteem

I would describe some aspects of my own self-esteem as being negative rather than low. It is in relation to other people that I feel so much shame about how I might appear to them and about not being able to be one of them and relate to them in any kind of 'normal' way.

Me

As a consequence of my difficulties not being recognised or understood either by myself or by those around me for 37 years of my life, I have spent much of my adult life feeling that I have a negative value. Not understanding why I am the way that I am, I have felt so abnormal, and so different from other people that I didn't really count myself as part of the human race at all. When I am alone, the difficulty that I have in relating to other people doesn't matter.

Recently being diagnosed and realising that it is the reason why I am different to the majority of people has given me the chance to understand things about myself. Suddenly things about myself that have never made sense before have started to make a lot of sense. Finally having the chance to understand why I am the way that I am is gradually giving me the freedom and the confidence to believe in my right to be myself and to express myself in my own unique way, where previously I didn't feel that I had any rights at all.

It also affects my ability to process language as quickly as others. This means I need to ask for repetition or clarification more than others. Similarly, because it takes time to process language, I may not be able to think of a quick response, or I might come out with it at the wrong time. (Yes, a cracked CD.)

'Information overload' causes me anxiety, as I find it difficult to process the language, body language, use of metaphor and idiom fast enough and think through appropriate responses. The anxiety is likely to make me come out with something to respond and it may sound abrupt, or I may talk over someone. There are topics in which I feel comfortable conversing; however, social 'chit-chat' makes me feel uncomfortable. Withdrawal then becomes a way of dealing with it.

The social challenge: what young people tell us

This personal account of the fear and anxiety felt when required to be among other human beings is an experience that many people with ASD endure. Research has shown that people with ASD do not 'tune in' to how others are thinking or feeling in the same intuitive way as the majority of people (Baron-Cohen et al., 2000). As a consequence they struggle to make sense of other people's words and actions and are confused about how they are expected to behave towards them. Children with High Functioning ASD may be eventually able to work out how other people are thinking but it takes a great deal of effort and conscious analysing in comparison to the more instinctive reactions of most people.

Autistic Spectrum Disorder

The difficulties which people with ASD experience in 'tuning in' to what other people are thinking is compounded by the problems they have in their use and understanding of language.

Children with High Functioning ASD can be expected to develop enough expressive and receptive language skills to cope with straightforward everyday situations (although some are late to speak). Nevertheless, they can continue to experience difficulties in starting conversations, taking turns and maintaining a topic. Often there are problems with understanding verbal information, and remembering a sequence of instructions.

It is very common for children on the autistic spectrum continuum to be confused when someone says something which can only be truly understood by placing their words in a social context (Happe, 1994). For example, they may interpret sarcasm or figures of speech such as 'driving me round the bend' literally.

> I have a problem with metaphors and stuff, all those things you say but don't mean – like sometimes a kid might say, 'Oh yeah, I really love homework' when what they mean is 'I really hate homework'. It is difficult sometimes. It annoys me that people can't just say what they mean.
>
> *Year 6 pupil*

Pupils with High Functioning ASD find the social demands of school life extremely challenging. Adults need to respect that for these pupils, socialising with other children, particularly at playtime, is often not a pleasurable, relaxing or even positive experience.

While many children welcome the relative lack of structure and freedom offered by the playground, children with High Functioning ASD are frequently left feeling bewildered and confused. Some react by withdrawing themselves as far as possible from any kind of social interaction, finding solitude as a way of avoiding difficult situations and also as an opportunity to recover from the pressures of social conformity within the classroom. One pupil told me that secondary school was better than primary school because there were more places he could find to be on his own.

Certainly, when given the option, pupils with ASD will often volunteer to remove themselves from the playground in order to spend their time in more secluded environments where they can engage in activities by themselves or with one or two other children.

> I hate going out on the playground. I don't know what I am supposed to do and it is very cold. I told my mum I could take my PlayStation 2 to school but she said it wasn't allowed so what am I supposed to do?
>
> *Year 4 pupil*

For other children being on their own is not a choice but is something imposed on them by the reaction of other children. They are very keen to join in the play of their peers and to establish friendships but are constantly frustrated when their social approaches are continuously rebuffed. They look to adults to help them understand why this happens and what they can do about it.

> *Sometimes I know I have upset other kids and I don't know why. I know it is something I have said or done. They tell me to go away and tell the teacher I'm bothering them. But all I want to know is what I have done wrong.*
>
> *Year 5 pupil*

> *I want to play with other children but they say I can't play with them. I am sad when they say this. Sometimes they will play with me but lots of times they say no. I tell on them but Miss says they don't have to play with me if they don't want to.*
>
> *Year 3 pupil*

Children with ASD can often feel they are bullied and in some cases, this can result from a social misunderstanding. For example, the child may misread the intent of another child who accidentally knocks into them or tries to engage them in boisterous play (Attwood, 2004).

Anecdotal evidence as well as research (Thompson et al., 2001) suggests that children with ASD are frequently victims of intentional and systematic bullying. Clare Sainsbury's book *Martian in the Playground* (2000), for example, contains several disturbing accounts from people with ASD about being bullied at school, while a recent study (Attwood, 2004) indicated that children with High Functioning ASD are four times more likely to be bullied than their peers.

> *I call my primary school Hell on Earth. Every playtime a gang of other children would wait for me. They called me names and pushed me. This teacher found me once crying and she said, 'Just ignore them and they will leave you alone'. I didn't understand what she was talking about. Did she think I went out of my way to find them and ask them to bully me? I wish I could ignore them. She told the other kids off and one of them said if I told a teacher again, he would kill me. I believed he really would kill me and I used to lie in bed at night thinking about how he planned to do it.*
>
> *Year 8 pupil*

As well as experiencing difficulties with peer interactions, relationships with teachers or other adults can sometimes also be difficult. School staff may misunderstand the child's behaviour and view it as naughty, selfish, rude, difficult or lazy, when in fact the child may not have understood the situation or task or did not read the adult's intentions or mood correctly. Children with ASD often do not have an intuitive grasp of social hierarchy and it may not occur to them that they are expected to treat somebody in a special 'respectful' way just because that 'somebody' is a teacher.

> *We had this supply teacher once in primary school. She was very fat. I remember seeing a television programme that said that fat people were more at risk of dying.*

I thought she may not have seen this programme and I ought to tell her about it. So I started telling her that she was very fat and that was because she ate too much. I never got to finish what I wanted to say because she got very angry and I got into lots of trouble. I didn't know what I had done wrong because I had just told the truth.

Year 8 pupil

The social challenge: what we can do about it

Teaching social conformity: behaviour plan

In order to improve a child's social skills, staff often aim to change those behaviours which have a negative impact on the child's interactions with adults and peers. One way in which this can be done is by introducing a behaviour plan (Whitaker, 2001). This involves identifying (in as specific terms as possible) the 'unwanted' behaviour and also the alternative 'desired' behaviour.

The child is then prompted to demonstrate the 'desired' behaviour, which is then immediately rewarded by a 'reinforcer' (stickers, verbal praise, access to a favourite activity, etc.). On the other hand, the 'unwanted' behaviour is ignored or reinforcers removed or denied.

The prompts and reinforcers are then gradually phased out in the hope that the 'desired' behaviour will become incorporated into the child's independent everyday interactions. Such an approach can be a very powerful tool in helping a child learn to conform to basic social expectations.

Nevertheless, using a behaviour plan to encourage social competence can have its limitations if the child does not have an understanding of why they are been encouraged to behave in a certain way. For example, a behaviour plan might teach a child not to snatch things from others but the child may comply because the child wants stickers and not because the child has any understanding of why 'snatching' is socially inappropriate. The child therefore may revert to the problem behaviour when the stickers are no longer given out or when supervised by a different adult. For this reason it is important to teach the child social understanding alongside social conformity.

Teaching social understanding: Social Stories

What children with ASD want is to be provided with clear information about how our social world works in a format which is accessible to them. For the majority of people our brains work in such a way that many of these things seem obvious. It may be hard for us to understand how a child doesn't automatically know these things, particularly if the child seems able in other areas. It is important to rid ourselves of this assumption and realise that what we need to do is bridge a gap between our social understanding and the social understanding of the child.

One powerful strategy developed by Carol Gray is the use of Social Stories (Gray, 1999). This involves writing a short passage which describes a particular social situation. A social story does not aim to instruct a child but rather to provide the child with the key information, which they may not instinctively 'pick up' for themselves. It should be written following the guidelines that Gray has developed to ensure that it has a supportive, reassuring quality. The story can then be read to the child at regular intervals or they can read it themselves.

Another important point to remember is that Social Stories have another purpose that is equally important – acknowledging achievement. Written praise may be far more meaningful for children with ASD than its verbal counterpart. At least half of the Social Stories written for a child with ASD, and especially the first one, should address positive achievements.

I have visited schools where teachers tell me that Social Stories worked really well at first but that now every time the child is shown a Social Story, the child becomes distressed. This usually means that Social Stories have been used only when the child has done something wrong or when there has been a problem. The child has therefore learnt to associate Social Stories with something negative and not surprisingly has learnt to hate them. This could have been avoided if Social Stories had also been used to celebrate, especially initially, what the child could do well.

Example of Social Stories written by staff at River Bank School

At lunchtime

In the dinner hall, children who have packed lunches sit on one side, and children who have school dinners sit on the other side. This makes it easier for the dinner ladies to look after the children. When the children go to lunch, they should sit at the next empty place. Sometimes children will have to sit next to people who are noisy, or who talk with their mouth open. If this happens, the children should try to ignore them and talk with the people they do get on with.

On the carpet

When Miss N. calls us to the carpet, it is because she has something to share with the whole class. If everyone sits together and close to Miss N., everyone can see and hear properly. Miss N. is happy when this happens because she can help everyone learn. It doesn't matter who we sit with on the carpet. Sometimes children have to sit near people they are not friends with. If this happens, the children should be sensible and just pay attention to Miss N. Miss N. will be pleased and will be able to teach the class without people interrupting.

Teaching social understanding: Comic Strip Conversations

Another strategy devised by Carol Gray is the use of Comic Strip Conversations (Gray, 1999). This helps the child to think about a difficult incident they have experienced by encouraging them to draw what happened using stick figures with speech bubbles and thought bubbles. Emotions such as anger or fear are represented by the use of different colours. This superficially simple technique encourages the child not merely to review what happened but also to gain a better understanding of what other people might have been thinking or feeling at the time.

Rehearsing social situations

Some pupils like the opportunity to rehearse a difficult or challenging social situation through the use of role play, perhaps with an adult or with other children in a small group. They may benefit from being provided with a social script which gives them some ideas of the kinds of phrases which might be helpful for them to use in particular situations.

Evidence suggests that individuals may not easily make links between the work they do in a social skills group and the real setting. Care needs to be taken to ensure that the child transfers the skills learnt in the social skills group into the classroom and the playground (Ozonoff and Miller, 1995).

Case study: social skills group

In the following account the head teacher and SENCO at Peachtree Primary describe the setting up of a social skills group.

As teachers we assume that as a by-product of being in a school environment all children will acquire the social skills that they need in order to operate successfully in school, access the curriculum and, more importantly, operate in society. While this may be true for the vast majority of children there are some who require more explicit teaching of social skills, particularly those with a diagnosis of ASD. I was involved in teaching children with ASD in a previous post as a peripatetic teacher. When I came to this school it became apparent that there were lots of children who were constantly missing playtimes because of their inappropriate behaviour. A large percentage of these children were boys and they were also, on the whole, well behaved in class.

I began by running a few social skills groups with a teaching assistant (TA) and I chose four children who needed to develop their skills and four or five others who could model good skills. It is important to get the balance right and choose the groups carefully as this will determine whether the group is likely to be a success. Children acquire most of their behavioural traits from their significant others by mimicking and their peers can be extremely influential in this process.

Since it was clear very early on in my appointment that there was a need for a range of social skills groups to be run across the school, I conducted a training session with all the TAs and

---

(Continued)

they were given guidance on how to run the sessions. All the sessions follow a pattern and the focus is to develop good listening, looking, thinking, concentrating and speaking skills. The sessions also involve turn taking and co-operation. The children all begin by greeting each other and end by saying goodbye. The sessions must have a clear structure and this will be determined by the skills you wish to develop.

The TAs and I have put together a bag of interesting objects (for sharing) and there are currently seven social skills groups in operation throughout the school. The next stage is to develop the sessions by observing each other and by adding new games to our repertoire of activities. One of the TAs suggested the children should shake hands with each other at the end of each session and this strategy has been incorporated into the practice of other TAs and myself.

The impact of the social skills groups on improving behaviour throughout the school has been significant and the TAs also consider they have been empowered with new skills. The full impact of the sessions, however, may take a while to materialise as it can take many months to change or modify behaviour so it is important to be patient. Success is evident when you see children in the playground asking each other how they are and saying how much they enjoy playing games with one another and this can then be celebrated during Circle Time.

Teaching emotions

In the personal account at the beginning of this chaper, there is a description of how other people's emotional state is often a 'complete mystery' to a person with ASD because of their problems in interpreting facial expressions and tone of voice. This can be addressed by explicitly teaching the pupil about different emotions and how they are expressed.

Initially, the child should be introduced to the four basic emotions of happiness, sadness, anger and fear. The child can be taught to recognise the basic facial expressions associated with these feelings in cartoons, photographs and videos. The book *Teaching Children with Autism to Mind-Read* (Howlin et al., 1999) provides a practical approach to helping children identify how an emotion can be triggered by a person's understanding of a situation. It is important, however, that the child is also encouraged by adults to appreciate how this relates to 'real life'. This can be done by, for example, using a commentary to draw the child's attention to how another child is feeling and why, e.g. 'Look at John's face. John is sad because you pushed him', or 'Jane is happy because she likes playing with the sand'.

As children get older they can be introduced to the vocabulary used to describe more complex and subtle emotions. One strategy can be to show a child a video with the sound turned down and then ask them to interpret what is going on, by 'reading' the characters' body language. The child could also create books about different emotions and use a thermometer-like scale to measure their own emotional reactions (Attwood, 2004). Older children can benefit by being taught to 'read' body language, for example to recognise the 'tell-tale' signs that suggest that someone is bored or fed up.

Addressing the issue of playtime

Consideration needs to be given to 'playtime' as a whole-school issue. The idea of sending children out to play without any clear structure, often under the supervision of staff who have minimal training in special educational needs (SEN), clearly doesn't work for children with ASD. There is a need to address the issue at a whole-school organisational level. Quentin (2003), as a result of an investigation into the playground experiences of pupils with disabilities, suggests that strategies to improve playtimes may include:

‣ Staggering breaktimes to reduce crowding.

‣ Zoning the playground according to activity or age groups.

‣ Reducing the length of playtimes or removing afternoon break.

‣ Organising breaktime activites and investing time in teaching children how to play traditional games which have clear rules and a repetitive structure.

‣ Improving the playground environment by organising seating and equipment in order to direct the children to certain activities.

For some children alternative arrangements to going out on the playground may need to be put in place. For example, the child could be encouraged to stay in the classroom with one or two children and play a board game, read books or use the computer. The child with ASD may need some solitary time to 'refuel their batteries' because they find social contact both tiring and stressful. It might be possible to start up a club related to the child's special interests or give the child a role such as library monitor. Some schools provide a room or base in which a child can go to relax at planned times or in times of crisis (Barratt and Thomas, 1999).

Providing lunchtime support for pupils at Lake Side High School

At Lake Side High School, children with ASD know that they can go to M10, a room in the SEN Department before school, at breaks and at lunchtime where there is access to computers and other resources. Although on Friday lunchtimes students are required to sit down and participate in a formal lunch, to a great extent the students pursue their own choice of activity in M10.

One 'knock on' effect of these arrangements is that the young people have developed a sense of identity as a 'group' and therefore feel more confident about having ASD.

> Going to M10 allows me to touch base. It has proved a great asset. If I need to go there, I can. It is a contingency plan. Since I've become aware of my difficulties I want to live my life normally but it is useful in an emergency.

> Sometimes I do and sometimes I go to the library. It is a good idea though. It is a lot easier to relate to other people with Asperger's syndrome. With kids who don't have it

you have to think more about what you say. People without Asperger's get upset very easily, like if you say something in the wrong tone of voice. We have our own sense of humour and get each other's jokes.

I sometimes go to M10 and sometimes the playground. You can get on with your homework and I once organised a draughts competition. It is a useful arrangement to have M10.

I get on with other students with Asperger's syndrome. My best friend doesn't have Asperger's syndrome but he understands where I am coming from. But if I have a problem it is best to talk to another person with ASD because they can see my point of view.

Children with ASD can often feel distressed that they do not have 'friends'. If an adult can create a situation in which other children are willing to participate in a shared activity, then the child with ASD may perceive the other children as 'friends' even if some of the more subtle characteristics associated with friendships may be absent.

Because of the difficulties Xavier had at playtime we decided to allow him to stay in the classroom at playtimes. He was allowed to pick two other children to stay with him. Other children were keen to stay in and especially during the winter months. He became extremely popular.

Year 4 class teacher

Circle of Friends

If a child is becoming socially isolated, peer support strategies can be used to teach the child with ASD to be more assertive. Consideration also needs to be given to educating other children about their classmate's difficulties and encouraging them to play a supportive role. Changing the behaviour of other children may prove more effective than teaching the child with ASD on how to manage being isolated and ignored (Jones, 2002).

I think other children should be taught about people like me. Some kids say I am thick. I know I am not thick and I try to explain this to them but they don't listen. If you are different, you are seen as wrong.

Year 9 pupil

One strategy that has been designed to create a peer support network and has been used successfully with children with ASD (Whitaker et al., 1998) is the Circle of Friends approach.

Autistic Spectrum Disorder

Circle of Friends

Circle of Friends is an inclusive approach which involves enlisting the support of the peer group to change the behaviour of a focus pupil. Peer support offered through Circle of Friends can be an extremely effective strategy for addressing pupils' social needs.

The following case study relates to a secondary school student with Asperger's syndrome. Before transferring to a mainstream secondary school Tom attended a special school. The Circle of Friends approach was introduced when Tom was in Year 8.

Parental permission

The SENCO initially discussed the possibility of implementing Circle of Friends with both Tom and his parents. The strategy was outlined and, following a positive response from both Tom and his parents, the form tutor became involved and six students (three boys and three girls) became Tom's Circle of Friends. A training programme was set up for these students. In addition to seeking permission from Tom's parents, the parents of the other six students in the Circle were also contacted by the school and it was explained that these students would be involved in a peer support strategy. Positive feedback was received from the parents of students in the Circle.

Training

The SENCO conducted a meeting with the six students who had volunteered to be in the Circle and a discussion was held on autism. Students within the group commented on some of Tom's social behaviours and suggested how they might help Tom to become less isolated.

Establishing the Circle

Following these initial steps, Tom subsequently joined the group for the next meeting. Thereafter, meetings of approximately 30 minutes took place on a fortnightly basis. These meetings enabled Tom to talk about issues he was trying to deal with and how the Circle might support him with them. Students in the Circle commented on Tom's strengths. The sessions were scheduled weekly in the latter part of either a Humanities lesson or a Modern Foreign Language lesson. The subject teachers involved were aware of the potential benefits of the Circle approach for Tom and were therefore supportive of the arrangement.

Positive Outcomes

Through the influence of the Circle, other students in the peer group gradually became more positive towards Tom and he began to return greetings. Tom agreed to bring in something interesting from home to talk about and share with the Circle in school, e.g. a computer magazine.

As the relationship developed between Tom and the six members of the Circle, he agreed to approach the Circle rather than them always relying on themselves to initiate contact. Two of the girls had lunch with Tom on a regular basis and as his confidence grew he agreed to spend all of the lunch hour on one day a week with his Circle, instead of immediately rushing off to the library. Through the intervention of the Circle Tom began to participate in more social activities at school, e.g. the drama festival.

During Years 8 and 9, Tom made good progress in terms of developing positive social relationships with his peers. In Year 10, however, because of option choices, Tom was not in the same teaching group as his Circle. He became withdrawn and therefore the Circle strategy was reactivated. However, after the first term in Year 10, regular meetings of the Circle were no longer needed.

Tom is now in Year 11 and is able to interact with his peers, to the extent that he chats with a student who used to tease him in Year 8. The SENCO reports that 'Circle of Friends' is an approach that has really worked for this vulnerable student. The Circle developed a range of skills and supported the 'focus' student and each other in a positive manner. Tom became much more confident and his social and emotional progress was enhanced. Tom is happy at school and his parents are enthusiastic about the peer support that he has received.

The 'Circle of Friends' approach has been developed further by the SENCO and as a result form tutors are now undertaking 'Circle of Friends' work with their groups. 'Circle of Friends' training materials have been made available throughout the school and staff consider that there has been a very high success rate with this strategy.

The learning environment: what young people tell us

Many people with ASD have extreme sensitivity to certain sights, sounds and textures (Grandin, 1995; Lawson, 1998; Sainsbury, 2000). As a result, a 'busy' classroom with lots of eye-catching displays, mobiles dangling from the ceiling and interesting items on show can be a sensory 'nightmare' for children with ASD and they can find it very difficult to screen out background distractions.

Children with ASD can often miss the 'clues' which other children intuitively pick up about what behaviour is required of them and how they are expected to interact with their environment.

Because the world can seem such a strange and bizarre place, children with ASD feel much calmer and relaxed when they are within a familiar, predictable environment. They may also find it hard to adapt to new situations and often get 'stuck' in a routine. They find it difficult to use their initiative and can find changes very challenging and upsetting (Sainsbury, 2000; Jones, 2002).

If there is one thing I would change about school, it is that there would be less room changes. It used to make me angry as I didn't understand why these room changes occurred and it seemed to me that they were just done to confuse the kids. I couldn't understand why they just couldn't stick to the timetable. My tutor has explained that there are very important reasons why these room changes are necessary. But I still don't like them. They unsettle me, especially when I am given very little warning.

Year 10 pupil

Happe (1994) suggests that people with ASD can be very proficient at tasks requiring attention to detail but that they struggle to make connections between these details in order to create a bigger picture. It is rather like a person becoming so focused on each separate piece of a jigsaw puzzle that they fail to appreciate how these pieces can be slotted together in order to complete the puzzle.

The expression 'can't see the wood for the trees' appears to be extremely apt when considering the difficulties children with ASD experience with learning. A focus on detail can help them to learn a particular skill but they may often not then realise how what they have learnt connects with previous learning experiences. As such their understanding can often be very fragmented. This failure to see the 'bigger picture' can result in difficulties in areas such as:

- ▸ extracting the relevant information to complete the task;
- ▸ understanding the purpose of an activity or how it relates to what has gone on before;
- ▸ working out what is relevant and what should be left out;
- ▸ putting things into an order or categorising them into groups;
- ▸ making inferences and predictions.

Children with ASD often become engrossed in a particular activity and want to repeat it over and over again. They may also become fascinated with a specific subject and may develop a remarkable degree of knowledge about it. Adults can become very concerned about these 'obsessions' because they feel they restrict the child's learning experiences and increase their social isolation. Nevertheless, it is very clear from talking to people with ASD that these 'special interests' provide a tremendous degree of comfort and reassurance and are a fixed reference point in a seemingly unpredictable and ever changing world.

Sometimes I obsess about stuff. I want to talk and talk about the same things over and over again. I do that a lot. I know I am doing it but I can't help myself. People say, "you just told me that a minute ago".

Year 10 pupil

Children with ASD tend to find it easier to cope with activities that involve rote learning or involve applying rules or understanding a system or structure rather than activities that require spontaneity, independence or creativity (Powell, 2000). For example, in literacy a child with ASD often shows relative strengths in reading phonetically or applying spelling rules but struggles with comprehension, inference and creative writing. In numeracy children with ASD may find it easy to learn multiplication tables but may not be able to apply this knowledge to solve numerical problems. They tend to be more successful in academic areas that do not require high degrees of social understanding and where the language used is technical or mathematical (for example, science and information technology).

Children with High Functioning ASD can have problems processing spoken language. These difficulties may not be obvious because the child's verbal fluency can mask them. Furthermore, children with ASD often answer 'yes' to any question they do not understand as a means of ending a confusing and stressful conversation (Wing, 1981).

> *I find that teachers talk too much ... talking and talking ... and I lose some of the stuff they said at the start. Sometimes they tell you to copy something and they carry on talking to you and you don't know whether to listen or write. If you get something wrong, it stops you writing but they keep talking and talking.*
>
> *Sometimes when I ask they just come out with a channel of words. Then when they have finished they say, 'Do you understand now?' So I nod because I am afraid they will just keep talking.*
>
> *Year 9 pupil*

Pupils with ASD are generally more able to process information which is written (or presented in other visual means) rather than that which is presented orally. They are often classified as visual learners although it is important to appreciate that the visual information – whether text, pictures, diagrams or tables – still has to be presented is a straightforward, simple format if the pupils are required to extract meaning.

> *I wish teachers would make it clearer what they want me to do. If they made it clearer, I wouldn't mess it up and I would do it right. Most teachers don't make it clear enough. The worksheets are sometimes hard to understand. They should make them clearer.*
>
> *Year 10 pupil*

While no child enjoys getting things wrong, children with ASD seem to find it very difficult to persevere with a task if they do not experience immediate success. They will often make considerable efforts to avoid repeating the task again. They may have difficulty understanding what they are being asked to do or what the point of an activity is and therefore can sometimes appear to be very poorly motivated.

The learning environment: what we can do about it

Classroom arrangements and seating plans

An approach which many children with ASD can benefit from is TEACCH (Treatment and Education of Autistic and related Communication –

handicapped Children) (Mesbov and Howley, 2003). This approach emphasises setting up structured learning environments with minimal distractions and building on the child's visual strengths. This approach can be incorporated into mainstream classrooms.

Staff need to be aware of how a child's sensory reactions can significantly impact on their ability to focus and stay calm within the classroom. It may not be necessary or desirable to create a completely distraction-free environment with blank walls and no pictures. Nevertheless, children with ASD can work far more effectively in a mainstream classroom with fewer distractions and only minor changes to the physical environment (Jones, 2002). Teachers may consider limiting displays to specific areas of the classroom, placing items in storage boxes or cupboards and using screens or other furniture to 'hide' distractors from the child's view.

It is important within this approach to pay particular attention to the space around where the pupil sits. Establishing a seating plan for the whole class and using photographs and labels to reinforce where children are required to sit can be very helpful. It is often best to position the child with ASD near the front of the class, facing the board, away from 'traffic routes' and alongside children who provide good models of behaviour.

Children with ASD can find it difficult to concentrate when sitting in close proximity to other children. It is important to give the child as much 'personal space' as the classroom permits and use tape to clearly mark out the boundaries of the child's work area.

Some children who are very distracted and unfocused when required to work independently may find it helpful to sit on their own. Ideally this should be on a table facing a blank wall away from any distractions and possibly screened off from the rest of the class. It is helpful to ensure that the equipment the child needs for the lesson is available before the lesson starts. The aim is to build an association between the location and getting down to work. At other times the pupil can be moved nearer to their peers for group and partner work. (Care should be taken to ensure that the pupil doesn't end up spending long periods of time isolated from the other children or that the child perceives being in the low distraction zone as a punishment.)

Many children with ASD benefit from a 'time out' arrangement which allows them to go to a quiet area to relax and de-stress.

If the class are required to sit on the carpet area, make sure that the pupil has a regular spot marked with tape or a carpet tile. Consider allowing the pupil to sit on a chair at the edge of the carpet area.

When children are required to line up have them line up in the same order.

Children with ASD can find sharing equipment very difficult so it might be a good idea to avoid the pupil having to share by providing them with their own labelled materials and equipment. The pupil can then be gradually taught how to take turns.

To help the child understand how the classroom is organised, mark storage areas, containers and cupboards with pictures and labels.

Visual timetables

Put symbols and words on cards to represent the main activities of the day. Stick the cards on a board or on the wall using Blu-tack or Velcro in order to create a simple visual timetable. As each activity is completed remove the relevant card and 'post' it in a box or plastic wallet. Make reference to the timetable throughout the school day ('Look at the timetable. Can anyone tell me what we are going to be doing after lunch?'). Have a visual cue to indicate a change of routine, such as a gold star or a different coloured card.

For many children with ASD, a whole-class timetable is enough to help the child understand the daily routine and to prepare them for changes. Nevertheless, some pupils may require their own individual 'miniature' version of the mainstream timetable which can be placed on their desk or on the wall near to their seat. The child should be trained how to use the timetable.

Introduce 'catchphrases' into the daily routine – things that you always say at particular times of the day, for example 'Freeze please ... carpet time'.

Establish 'transition' routines which warn children when activities are ending or about to end, for example ring a bell once five minutes before an activity finishes and then ring it twice when it finishes.

At the start of the day and after lunchtime, I always look at the timetable. I know what it says but I still like to check it to make sure that there are no surprises. It helps me feel a bit more relaxed and in control.

Year 5 pupil

Spelling out the rules

Although teachers have an expectation about how they want children to behave in their classroom, their expectations are often not explicitly stated. Teachers may be uncomfortable about stating the 'rules' or may express them in vague abstract terms, for example 'In our classroom, we try to remember to be nice to each other'. Children with ASD often find it easier to cope when behavioural expectations are expressed in a specific, clear and unambiguous way (Whitaker, 2001). This sometimes may be difficult because there may be no hard or fast rules. Nevertheless, children with ASD find it easier to understand social behaviour if it is expressed as a 'rule' or as a statement of fact about what everyone should do. A restrictive rule can be introduced but then gradually relaxed as children show they are able to conform to the rule. The focus on doing it because the 'rule' says so, rather than doing it because 'I tell you', can help reduce direct conflict between the adult and the child.

It is often a good idea to find a way of expressing the rule in some visual format. Symbols can be used or a list of rules can be written down or explained using a Social Story.

Visual strategy to support a behaviour rule

At Nighingale Primary School, a boy with ASD in a reception class would often walk out of the classroom and then run away. Staff realised that the situation was confused as children were allowed to leave the classroom to go to the toilet. It was decided to put red tape on the floor to mark the limits to how far pupils were permitted to go down the corridor.

Language

If the child with ASD appears confused or does not do what you ask, speak LESS rather than MORE. Speak clearly and slowly. Stress key words. Repeat instructions rather than rephrasing them. This is particularly relevant when the child is stressed or agitated. ('*Sit* down. *Draw* a picture of a dinosaur' rather than 'Do you think you could sit down now? Then perhaps you could draw me a nice picture of a dinosaur.')

Teachers often rush what they are saying. I wish they would speak more slowly or write things down for me.

Year 8 pupil

Tell the child exactly what you want them to do. If the child can read, write down what you want them to do on a 'post-it' and leave it with the child.

If pupils have been taught new vocabulary outside of the classroom, perhaps by following a speech and language programme, it is important that situations are created within the classroom to encourage them to use the words they have learnt in the 'real' world. Children with ASD can learn words by rote but will not necessarily incorporate them into their everyday speech without encouragement.

Children can also benefit from developing speech and language skills within a structured framework such as the 'Talking Partners' programme (Kotler et al., 2001). Be aware of potential confusion created when using idioms, double meanings and sarcasm, as well as vague terms like 'maybe' or 'perhaps'. Nevertheless, the child may benefit from an adult explicitly introducing them to everyday figures of speech. ('We can't go out to play today Imran because it is raining cats and dogs outside. That is something people say when it is raining heavily but of course it isn't really raining cats and dogs.')

I keep a list of figures of speech in a notebook. My teacher told me to collect them. They are very silly and quite funny. My favourite is 'kick the bucket'.

Year 10 pupil

It is important that language is matched to the child's level of understanding. Some children with ASD can develop an extensive vocabulary and can incorporate quite sophisticated language into their everyday speech. They can often also demonstrate an impressive factual recall. Adults, however, need to be aware that this may mask significant gaps in their comprehension of what is being said to them. The child may have no difficulty in repeating what they have heard even if they don't understand the meaning of what they are imitating. Often they will reply 'yes' to a question which confuses them or when asked if they understand (Wing, 1981).

At times when the child is angry or distressed, save reasoning and explanation for later.

Work systems and other ways of structuring work

Children with ASD can struggle with open-ended activities or with being given too many choices or options. They tend to learn best when materials are presented in a structured, sequential format, for example lists, multiple choices, etc. Expectations about quantity and quality of work output need to be explicit and detailed ('Write *three* reasons why the Romans wanted to invade Britain' rather than 'Why do you think the Romans invaded Britain?'). It may also be helpful for the pupil to see examples of finished work from other pupils.

Left to their own devices, pupils will have difficulty identifying where to begin and end a task and how to organise their time. If they are given individual support and a high level of prompting and encouragement, it may be possible to get them to complete a task, but this does not encourage the child to work independently.

In such cases, it may be relevant to introduce a work system. This encourages a child to work in a particular way, using a predictable, methodical, consistent approach to tasks. It takes advantage of the child with ASD's need for routine (Mesbov and Howley, 2003).

A work system should present a task in such a way as the child can clearly understand the answer to four key questions:

▶ What work do I have to do?

▶ How much work?

▶ How do I know when I am finished?

▶ What happens next?

Work systems can be incorporated into the regular class activities. They need to be tailored to the level of independence and academic ability of the child.

The simplest system would consist of an individual activity box, which contains all the items needed for an activity. The box is placed on the left-hand side of the table. The child opens the box, completes the task and then places the box

Autistic Spectrum Disorder

in a finished tray on the right-hand side of the table. The child then picks up the reward card and gives it to an adult.

When the child can easily complete one activity box without supervision, more boxes can be added.

Some children may not need such a high level of structure but will benefit from being given a 'task planner'.

Once the child has developed reading skills, the information can be presented to them in the form of a simple 'to do' list. The aim should be for the child to eventually be able to organise themselves by creating their own checklist or task planner.

> *My helper writes down a list of what I've got to do in the lesson and I tick it off as I do it. This really helps. My old helper used to talk to me all the time. She was talking in one ear and the teacher was talking in the other ear.*
>
> *Year 5 pupil*

> *I forget things very easily. My brain is like that cheese that has holes in it. My teacher told me to write lists to help me remember. It really helps me.*
>
> *Year 11 pupil*

The use of a sand timer or stop watch with an alarm may help the pupil develop a sense of time passing in lessons. Targets to develop the child's concentration could focus around completing a set amount of work before the sand runs out or the alarm sounds.

If the pupil is required to produce extended writing, the pupil may need help in structuring work, for example, writing frames, mind maps, etc. Pupils with ASD may need to be provided with opportunities to show knowledge and understanding of topics in ways that require little or no writing. Alternatives which can be explored include computer, tape recorder, dictating, cut and stick, cloze procedures and 'tick the correct box' activities.

It can be possible to address certain areas of the curriculum through the pupil's 'special interests'. It is also worth trying to use any special interest as a source of reward and motivation, for example, 'If you complete this work by 10:30, then you can get ten minutes to work on your space project.' Access to computers can be a particularly effective strategy for the child with ASD as they are visual, predictable, can be controlled and make no social demands (Murray, 1997).

Group work can be very difficult for children with ASD. Consideration could be given to letting the child work by themselves or perhaps with one friend. Otherwise, the group activity needs be extremely well structured to ensure that the child is very clear about their role. The pupil may benefit from pre-teaching from a TA before joining a group activity.

Anxieties should be recognised and, if possible, pressure reduced in these situations. Be aware of possible additional stress factors such as increased noise and movement levels and loss of security through the lack of understanding of what might be happening.

Teaching reading: reciprocal teaching

Some children with ASD experience difficulties in learning to read. In such cases it may be useful to use a 'whole word' approach, starting with familiar words and words which relate to the child's interest (Hannah, 2001). Many children can read accurately, in the sense of decoding fluently, but cannot understand a lot of what they read. As many as 30–50 per cent of children with High Functioning ASD are hyperlexic and can read well in advance of their understanding (Jones, 2002).

It is therefore important not to make assumptions about a child's understanding of a text based on their ability to decode words. Children with ASD may also need to be explicitly taught the strategies required in order to comprehend a text. The 'Reciprocal Teaching Method' (Palincsar and Brown, 1984) is one approach which aims to do this by teaching a child to follow four key strategies when reading a passage of text:

▸ Predicting – using clues to work out what the author will discuss next.

▸ Clarifying – checking for any gaps in understanding and, if necessary, rereading parts of the text.

▸ Questioning – asking questions about the text based on who, what, why, where, which, when and how.

▸ Summarising – identifying the main ideas in the text.

Curriculum access for a pupil with ASD within a nursery setting

When Sam first started at the nursery he would just run from activity to activity. Any child who was in his way and didn't move fast enough was pushed aside. If adults tried to direct Sam, he would become agitated and aggressive, screaming at them 'Stupid! Stupid!' and pushing them away.

Structured routine and restricted choices

The staff concluded that Sam found the range and choice of activities available to him bewildering. It was decided to withdraw the choices and encourage Sam to follow a programme of carefully chosen activities in the same order each day. The TA would take Sam's hand and direct him through the programme of activities. Initially, the TA had to adopt a firm approach with

(*Continued*)

Sam to ensure that he kept to the routine, but in time Sam became more accepting of it. Gradually a wider range of activities were carefully introduced although the choices were still limited. This enabled Sam to enjoy a greater level of inclusion into the main nursery. The TA commented:

> Sam had been withdrawn from some activities to work in a small room attached to the nursery, but as he became more relaxed and settled into the routine it was possible to reduce the amount of withdrawal time.

A crucial factor in Sam's acceptance of the nursery routine was the introduction and consistent use of a visual timetable which enabled him to anticipate what would come next and thereby reduce his anxiety.

Communication

The TA commented:

> When Sam becomes anxious or upset he finds it difficult to process too much spoken information so a sign is more effective. I also have to speak more slowly when talking to Sam and repeat key phrases.

The TA also realised that saying 'no' to Sam was guaranteed to cause an adverse reaction. It would appear that Sam had come to associate 'no' with being made to do things he didn't want to do and with being told off! The TA therefore developed different ways of letting Sam know when he wasn't allowed to do something.

Staff also made sure that they gave Sam plenty of praise and reassurance to help him cope with his anxieties. A TA commented:

> If there was something Sam was afraid to touch, I would take it and stroke it in front of him saying things like 'It's OK' and 'It's lovely'. Eventually Sam would overcome his fear and join me.

Social interaction

Once Sam became more settled, his interaction with other children improved. He began to greet them, sit on the carpet next to them and join them in different activities. Sam began to develop his understanding of social rules so that he no longer snatches things or pushes children out of the way. Pictures have been used to help him recognise different facial expressions so that Sam can now begin to recognise when other pupils are sad or happy.

'Structured Teaching'

Another strategy that staff working with Sam found useful was Structured Teaching which was developed in the 1960s at the University of Carolina by Division TEACCH (Treatment and Education of Autistic and related Communication-handicapped CHildren). It was first introduced into the UK on a large scale in the 1990s. Structured Teaching places a tremendous effort on enabling children to learn to work without adult assistance or direct supervision. This is achieved by recognising and exploiting the strengths and preferred learning style of children with ASD – their need for routine and structure and their relative skills in processing visual information.

One strategy used in Structured Teaching is the creation of a work system that helps to organise specific work activities. They provide meaningful, organised and effective ways of carrying out specific tasks. The child with ASD is trained to use a system that enables them independently. Staff began to recognise that although Sam had made tremendous progress, they were constantly interacting with him to get him to complete tasks and he was not, therefore, developing independence. A work system was set up for Sam. It was a great success as staff report that Sam will now work through a series of learning activities by himself.

Impact

Sam will now play peacefully next to other children and when encouraged by adults will take turns. He is willing to accept adult directions and enjoys the company of adults. He appears a much calmer and happier child. The impact of ASD is still evident but there has been a significant transformation which is the direct result of the hard work and dedication of the school staff.

Conclusion

It is important to talk to children with ASD and find out how they feel and think and what they understand. This may prove to be a challenge because of their social communication needs. Nevertheless, it is worth making an effort because without establishing some insight into how these children understand and perceive their world our attempts to address their needs are unlikely to be successful. In the words of Jim Sinclair (1989):

Being autistic does not mean being inhuman. But it does mean being alien. It means that what is normal for other people is not normal for me, and what is normal for me is not normal for other people. In some ways I am terribly ill-equipped to survive in this world, like an extraterrestrial stranded without an orientation manual. But my personhood is intact. My selfhood is undamaged. I find great value and meaning in my life, and I have no wish to be cured of being myself. If you would help me, don't try to change me to fit your world. Don't try to confine me to some tiny part of the world that you can change to fit me. Grant me the dignity of meeting me on my own terms – recognize that we are equally alien to each other, that my ways of being are not merely damaged versions of yours. Question your assumptions. Define your terms. Work with me to build more bridges between us.

Useful websites

www.nas.org.uk

www.autism.org.uk/teachers

www.autism.org.uk/a-z

www.autism.org.uk/msms

www.teachernet.gov.uk/wholeschool/sen/teacherlearningassistant/asd/

www.teachernet.gov.uk/wholeschool/sen/asds/

www.drc.org.uk

www.dotheduty.org

www.autism.org.uk

www.info.autism.org.uk

Chapter 3

Including Pupils with Visual Impairment

Dr Ruth M. MacConville
Lisa Rhys-Davies

Introduction

The term 'visual impairment' refers to children who are classed as blind or have a significant loss of vision. The incidence of pupils with visual disability is very low. Overall there are an estimated 23,000 children in the UK and this figure includes those children with visual impairment and additional disabilities (often severe learning difficulties). Approximately 9,000 of the overall number of children with visual disability attend a local mainstream school. It is still fairly rare to find a child who is blind included in a mainstream school. It is estimated that across the UK there are about 840 children between the ages of 4 and 16 who use Braille, amounting to less than five per cent of all children with a visual impairment. Within each year-group of children in Britain there are likely to be approximately 70 children who use Braille and therefore may be described as being educationally blind (Clunies-Ross and Franklin, 1997).

Visual impairment covers a wide spectrum of loss of sight and includes a wide range of visual difficulties. There are many different eye conditions and sight can be affected in a myriad of different ways. Therefore it is important not to adopt a stereotypical view of those who have impaired vision. Visual impairment of any degree interacts in an unpredictable way with many factors that serve to differentiate individuals from each other. Each person will face individual challenges. In discussing children and young people with visual impairment it is important to emphasise that we are talking about a wide range of individuals all with different types and degrees of visual loss, all of whom have responded and adapted to their experiences in unique ways. This is highlighted in the two following personal accounts – one by a blind pupil, Nyron, and the second by a partially sighted boy called David. In the interests of confidentiality all names have been changed.

Personal accounts

Nyron

My name is Nyron. I am registered blind and I've been in mainstream school since nursery. I think mainstream schools are better than special schools because in a special school you'll be relying on everyone to do everything for you but in mainstream school you feel more normal and the same as everyone else.

I remember in nursery when there was a blue carpet. I ran someone over with a little toy car. I didn't know why I didn't see him. I just thought no one would have been able to see him.

I realised I was registered blind or partially sighted when I was being pulled out of class to be taught Braille. I was just wondering why I'm the only one who's learning Braille and then I realised I was partially sighted, or someone told me.

When I learnt Braille and started to use it I felt a bit different 'cos everyone's got pen and paper and I've just got this huge, great big, massive thing in front of me making a lot of noise. Afterwards everyone else got used to it and so did I. Then I felt it's not that bad. But I can still do handwriting. It's not quite as fast as Braille and not easy to read.

In Year 5 I had Miss H. as a support assistant. She was a Braille beginner. Braille was new to her at that time. I was having a spelling test. The last one that we had I got about two out of ten, so we done it again and I had the paper behind me with all the words on it. While she was asking me the words, I was reading it with my fingertips and looking at Miss H. so she didn't realise I was reading. She was saying, 'Very good, Nyron. Looks like you've done your homework.' But really I was just reading the words with my fingers.

When I was in Year 6 and got into high school, I was slightly scared 'cos I didn't know much about what it was going to be like and what to do. On the first day of school I didn't know where to go and what I was meant to do at first, but it wasn't long after I got used to it. Miss H. helped me learn where everything was in the school.

In primary school we didn't have uniforms so everyone just wore everything they wanted and I could find my friends easier because I could see the colour of whatever they're wearing, jumper or T-shirt or whatever, and at breaktime I just go on looking for that coloured jumper. But in high school everyone's got the same jumper so it's harder because everyone's wearing the same thing. I can't see the faces from afar, especially when it's bright. I tried to say to them 'I'll meet you in a certain place' but that didn't work because they'd forget. I mean they've got a lot of other things to do like meeting someone else, and I couldn't remind them – every day I couldn't say 'Don't forget to meet me there' cos I didn't see them.

Back in primary school I learnt touch typing because I couldn't see the keyboards and I was going right down, putting my head on the keyboard and Miss H. was sort of doing an impression of me and I found it quite funny. Now I don't look at the keyboard. Touch typing is about memorising the keyboard which I've been taught to do, so I can use that. I've got a laptop now which I use touch typing on and it is faster.

I've had mobility lessons and that helped me travel. First I learnt to travel from one point to another, like from my primary school to a certain post box. Then in high school I learnt how to get to and from school using two buses. Now I travel independently from school using two buses.

One time when me and my friend David was going home it was raining and the windows were really steaming so we could barely see out of them and we realised we'd missed our stop. So we got off the stop after and had to walk all the way back and that was 'cos you couldn't see nothing out of the windows. I like it that I can do everything that a sighted person could do including driving bikes. With reading print I use a magnifying glass.

Now just a couple of stories before I go. Firstly, in Year 9 we was in a big hall and I asked a girl out and she said 'yes', so she picked me up, kissed me and swung me around and then when she put me down I was kinda off balance and all over the place. I was so happy and also I couldn't see where I was. She forgot I was blind.

Second story: at lunchtime I have to have the same thing, the same food every day, which is pizza and chips, because I can't see what else is there. And I can't, you know, ask anyone what is there because everyone is in a rush at lunchtime and the queue's really long as it is and annoying. So people get irritated by the time they're having their lunch and by me holding them back by asking what's there will just annoy them even more. It's not 'cos they're being horrible to me. It's just irritating to everyone else.

Just to finish off, I really enjoy mainstream school. I wouldn't have preferred to go to a specialist school. You get a lot more independence here and you get treated the same as everyone else and there's lots of mates and lot of girls.

David

My name is David and I go to a high school and I'm in Year 10. I am partially sighted. I first realised I was partially sighted when I had a lot of people helping me and looking after me; that was in Reception. I do most things like ordinary people, like riding a bike, going to the cinema and swimming. When I was in primary school I learnt things to help me like touch typing. This benefits me to keep up with other children in the class. I have a laptop which I can do my homework and research on. I've been in high school for four years and I'm doing my GCSEs now. The laptop helps me a lot because I can't read my own handwriting and it helps me keep up with the other children so I don't get left behind.

At the moment I'm going to do work experience. I sent a letter to them not saying that I was partially sighted because they might say 'no' but I'm going to explain it on the phone to them.

I've been to a lot of things with the Royal National Institute of the Blind. The conference was one of them which showed me and my friend Nyron that there were other people with similar situations as us.

We had some problems in mainstream school because we couldn't find our friends on the playground because of the uniform; everyone's wearing the same jumper. We each got a Walkie Talkie and we switched it on at breaktime to try and find each other.

People sometimes get quite irritated when I'm looking for my change on the bus, especially the driver. Mainstream school is really good and I recommend it to visually impaired people. You get loads of other friends, not the same as you are, but just as individual, so I'm happy.

The social challenge: what young people tell us

What emerges from listening to pupils is an appreciation of the enormous amount of energy that they expend in school in order to be included. They are, in the words of Allan (1999), 'actively seeking inclusion' by continually working out how much demand they can make on the school situation without drawing unwanted attention to their disability. Pupils tell us that they prefer to minimise their day-to-day difficulties and get by on a reduced amount of information. They make choices not to access information: going right up to the board, using a magnifier, admitting to not being able to read a faded worksheet or see a shared book when doing so will draw unwanted attention to their visual disability.

> *In Science we were doing things on the computer and she [the teacher] was telling us how to do data logging. No, I couldn't see the screen. When Miss L. [science teacher] asked if I could see [the screen] I said 'yes'. I didn't want to use my magnifier in front of the others [pupils].*
>
> *Year 10 pupil*

Visual disabilities can potentially be a remover of self-esteem as constantly seeking to hide away a part of oneself has an adverse effect on confidence and self-worth.

> *We [pupils with visual impairment] lose street cred because of our sight. If we had their job [teacher] the kids would say, 'Look at her!' because we would have to go right up to the board to see it. My science teacher has got street cred; he can see the board. He hasn't got any problems.*
>
> *Year 9 pupil*

Avoiding being found out

The first thing we learn from talking to pupils with visual impairment, then, is that they do not want to be treated differently and may go to great lengths to avoid being 'found out'. Allan (1999) refers to this behaviour as 'a constant policing of boundaries around their own selves' (p. 47) and suggests that giving the impression of being sighted yet at the same time experiencing significant problems gives a quality of 'undecidability' (p. 47) to those with whom they come into contact, which means that pupils may become somewhat anonymous and isolated from the social milieu. Paradoxically, the situation is likely to be far more complex for pupils with moderate difficulties as they are more likely, on the face of it, to be able to get away with concealing their disability. Bauman (1964) wrote that pupils with partial sight show higher levels of anxiety and insecurity and can be misdiagnosed, misunderstood and socially isolated whereas the role of the blind is clearly defined. Those pupils with a less significant visual disability are more likely to be laughed at because they simply appear 'uncool' whereas those with a severe visual disability may well evoke understanding and even sympathy. Thompson et al. (2001) suggest that the majority of young people work hard to become very learned in the laws of cool because it is a code which helps them to navigate through the struggle of adolescence. Young people take coolness very seriously and pounce on difference. The strict code of cool usually boils down to the common denominator of looking 'right', wearing the 'right' brands and listening to the 'right' music. Pupils with visual disabilities may sometimes find it difficult to access the finely tuned rules of cool. They therefore stand out from their peers and are at risk of being teased and bullied in school (Thompson et al., 2001).

Looking different

Differences in appearance due to unusual physical characteristics are what Allan (1999) refers to as 'markers of a disability' (p. 57). There are many visual conditions which affect appearance. A child may have been born with albinism and have very white hair and skin. Albinism is a particular problem when children are from ethnic minorities, where skin and hair would otherwise be dark. Pupils may suffer nystagmus (rapid, involuntary eye movements) and have noticeably oscillating eyeballs – 'wobbly eyes'. A pupil with photophobia (a condition in which the eye cannot cope with too much bright light) may need to constantly wear sunglasses and a cap with a brim to provide a shield from sunlight. A pupil may have a visual prosthesis (glass eye) which can also be disturbing. Differences in appearance affecting the eyes–mouth region – 'the communication triangle' – can be particularly unsettling for others and pupils report that they receive stares and personal questions which generate strong feelings of shame and anger.

Low vision aids

Low vision aids (LVAs) also fall into the category of being 'markers of a disability' as they single a pupil out as being different from their peers. LVAs are individualised learning tools and include spectacles, binoculars and magnifiers, and even white canes. LVAs improve not only the individual's ability to read but also extend their visual environment, providing options for visual independence both during and after school hours (Mason, 1998). Pupils often tell us that they prefer not to use specialist equipment because controlling their peers' awareness of their disability by appearing to cope with everyday tasks would be spoiled if they were seen with a white cane or binoculars. This is not always the case, however. Harris (1998) emphasises that peer relationships are of primary importance to young people; hence when an LVA can provide access to an activity that is critical to being part of the group pupils will overcome their resistance to using specialist equipment. For example, Nyron, a Year 11 pupil, was so motivated to be included in the texting that was going on in his class that he began to use his magnifier openly for the first time in order to access messages.

Transition

We learn from listening to pupils that the period following entry to a new school is a critical time when pupils who stand out in any way from their peers are likely to be the target of questioning. Unless handled confidently, this questioning can lead to incidents of teasing and bullying.

> *Well it was very hard for me to start off with [in this school] because kids were coming up to me saying, 'Oh, can you see this?', 'Can you see this?'*

> *They asked me things like, 'How many fingers am I holding up?', 'What colour is this?', 'Am I sticking my tongue out at you?' I sort of ignored them and now they accept me. They leave me alone and now it is really nice in my class.*

> *Year 9 pupil*

> *Yeah and they asked me things too. 'Can you see my fingers?', 'What colour is this?', 'Can you see my writing?' And now they don't ask me any more questions. In the beginning they used to say, 'Why are you always wearing sunglasses and a hat?'*

> *Year 8 pupil*

Something to say

The amount of staring and the loss of anonymity of pupils who look different should not be underestimated. Rather than doing nothing or ignoring the unwanted attention, the most effective strategies for dealing with unwanted attention are those which acknowledge something is going on. Jane Frances (2004) describes, in her powerful book about children with facial disfigurement, the importance of being able to convert a person's uncertain, initial reaction to a disability into a more positive social interaction by 'having something to say'. A positive response and assertive body language can enable others to move beyond their initial, hesitant stance. School is an important social environment and the appropriate place for this training to occur, as being able to respond positively to people's reactions takes courage and practice.

Well it was a bit hard. I didn't know my way around the school; the kids were OK. Well, there was one or two silly little people taking the mick … There were also quite a lot of people who were asking me questions but I was happy to answer them … They asked me how far I could see and what exactly could I see in this face and stuff like that. I told them I could see the face but not the features and not the colours of the eyes and all that.

Year 7 pupil

This pupil explained to me that he had been happy to answer questions about his visual disability during his first weeks at high school because he considered his peers were being sincere and wanted to find out how his disability affects him. Some pupils seem to know instinctively that it is important to take questioning in their stride and recognise that if badly managed, such initial encounters can escalate into incidents of teasing and bullying which will be hidden from staff.

Jamie, now he is a bully. Do you remember – he used to bully Dave? Well, now he's started to bully me too. I was in the line at lunchtime and he [Jamie] just dashes in there and then he just kicked me in the nuts and then he said to me, 'That's what you'll get if you carry on the way you are'. He takes the mick out of my eyes and everything. When the teachers are around he pretends to be my best friend and then when they are gone he starts taking the mick out of my eyes again like saying, 'Oh make room for the blind boy, he needs a lot of space'.

Year 8 pupil

Understanding visual disability

We learn from listening to pupils that coming to terms with and understanding their disability is a continuous process that often starts in the primary school. Despite the wealth of literature available to support families during the period following diagnosis, pupils often report that they discovered that they have a visual impairment for themselves.

I didn't know [I was visually impaired] until I had to wear patches and all that – then I had support teachers and magnifying glasses and touch-typing lessons and all that. So I sort of found out for myself [that I was visually impaired].

Year 4 pupil

Terminology

Words are important. Parents are often concerned about the impact of the term 'blind' on their child and tell us that they prefer to use the term 'visual impairment'. Being described as 'blind' can therefore come as a shock to pupils when they hear it for the first time about themselves. Pupils report that events at high school such as obtaining a Freedom travel pass or a gym membership can bring them face to face often for the first time with the harsh terminology associated with their disability.

> We [pupils who are visually impaired] can get Freedom Passes. It means all buses and trains are free for us but why does mine say 'Registered Blind'? I'm not blind so why am I called 'Registered Blind'? Blind means you can see nothing at all and I can see a little bit so I'm partially sighted not blind.
>
> *Year 9 pupil*

Pupils tell us that the pleasure and pride of joining a gym can be seriously undermined by their dismay at realising their membership card labels them as disabled.

> I can't show this [gym membership card] to anyone. It's got 'Disabled' all over it. I hate that word. Why couldn't I just have a different coloured card or put 'D' after my name. I can't walk into the gym with anybody and take this [card] out. Disability could be anything. It could be learning problems, or adolescence [meaning autism]. I don't want anybody to think I've got those [disabilities]. If they have got to put something on the card, why can't they put 'visually impaired' not 'disability'.
>
> *Year 11 pupil*

> Because look, you are walking with your friends, yeah, and you go, 'Are you a member of a gym?' And the person said 'yeah' and then you go, 'So am I'. And then you go, 'Aah let me see your photo?' and then they go, 'Let me see your photo?' Then you show it to them and they go 'Duh! Look you are disabled'.
>
> *Year 10 pupil*

Social knowledge

In the previous chapter Stephen Dedridge explained that while many pupils welcome the relative lack of structure and freedom offered by the playground, children with ASD are often left feeling bewildered and confused at break times. Pupils with visual disabilities also tell us that they find the playground, especially in high schools, a threatening environment because of its sheer size. The fact that pupils are more likely to be wearing uniform also makes familiar faces difficult to locate.

> I've been so bored at lunchtime, I couldn't find any of my friends. I don't know, I just couldn't find any of them, I don't know where they were, I miss whole breaks looking for them all over the place. When I was in my primary school I would see my friend Andrew and I would remember to myself 'Oh yeah, he [Andrew] is wearing a yellow jumper today' – so later when I was in the playground I would look out for a yellow jumper to find Andrew. But in this [high] school I can't find any of my friends because it's [the playground] too big and they [pupils] are all wearing the same colour jumper.
>
> *Year 7 pupil*

Their peers report that pupils with visual disabilities become dependent upon them to tell them what is happening around them, especially in the playground:

> *Well he [pupil with visual impairment] can't see anything in the playground, man – I have to tell him where everything is. At lunchtime right, all day he's saying, 'What class is going in now?' and 'What's over there? What does that say?' and I go and tell him because he's too blind man and he can't see.*
>
> *Year 11 pupil*

An important factor in managing peer relationships is the pupil's ability to understand the social behaviour of others and 'read' social contexts. This becomes more critical as the pupil moves through high school and has to manage increasing independence.

> *Meeting girls, now that's the hardest thing in the world for me. I mean meeting girls is all right but then going a step further than that is hard. There's no way to solve it – she looks at me and smiles but how in hell am I meant to know she is even looking at me?*
>
> *Year 11 pupil*

Pupils with impaired vision may respond inappropriately as a result of missing visual detail such as eye contact, smiles, facial expression or gestures of others. The briefest interaction such as saying 'hi' to the 'wrong' person or 'ignoring' somebody you know well can be a source of social anxiety.

> *You say hello to the wrong person and everybody laughs …*
>
> *Year 7 pupil*

Pupils report that they have learnt from experience to avoid encounters rather than risk embarrassment. It can be stressful for pupils to negotiate the myriad of busy and challenging situations which occur in unstructured environments such as the playground.

> *I was walking across the playground and Glynn walked up to me and was walking with me, right, and there was a puddle and I walked into it and Glynn started cracking up – it was deep; he didn't tell me.*
>
> *Year 9 pupil*

Just as pupils with ASD prefer to seek out more structured settings during breaktimes so pupils with visual disabilities also report that they choose to spend breaks in places such as the library or the information and communications technology (ICT) suite. This is not only because the playground is large and it is

Visual Impairment

difficult to negotiate contact with peers; the playground is also where pupils are likely to be targeted for systematic bullying. Pupils report that drawing attention to themselves in lessons can lead to being bullied later in the playground.

> We was on the computers in Science and Miss [science teacher] was saying about the experiment – she connected something up on the 'login' so the computer was drawing the graph by itself and everybody was looking at it. I couldn't see a thing, but I pretended I could. I didn't want to get out my binoculars to see the screen 'cos sometimes then out of lessons I get … well people say things to me like 'You are not going to know if your girl is ugly', 'You are not going to know where to kiss her'.
>
> *Year 10 pupil*

Lunchtime

Pupils recognise that despite their status of being fully included in their mainstream school their disability nevertheless imposes certain intractable limits upon them. At lunchtime, for example, difficulties may arise, not only because of the difficulty of locating friends or somewhere to sit down, but also because pupils report that they are unable to see the menu. Pupils tell us that they frequently have difficulty managing their meals. Allan (1999) provides a moving account of a 'mistake' made by a 14-year-old pupil called Laura which typifies many of the incidents that pupils tell us about:

> There was a time when instead of pouring vinegar on my chips I actually poured the water from the flower vase on my chips. I could hear everybody stop eating and they were all looking at me, thinking 'what a shame', I could tell. I just wanted to disappear.
>
> *(p. 50)*

Travel

For many pupils, being able to travel to school in the same way as their peers is vital.

> My dad, he just made me so angry – he made me go in the minicab again, you know the one that stinks of tar, and he made me go in it again. Better be the last day you know. It was because it was cold. I was going to say to him if it's cold, then does it mean I don't have to play out at breaktime? I haven't got the guts to be rude to my dad. But he gets me so annoyed this better be a one-off. I mean it 'cos I'm not going in that stinkin' little cab again.
>
> *Year 8 pupil*

One would assume that because pupils are keen to travel independently and catch the bus to school along with their peers they are therefore fully included in this aspect of school life. However, this is not necessarily the case.

I always come to school late. What happens is I can't see ahead. Most children know when there is a lot of traffic ahead of them but I don't. So most people tell me, 'Oh you might get to school late because there is a lot of traffic today'. Then all the other kids get off the bus and walk it or jog but I can't because I only know the way [to school] by not walking, so I have to put up with it. I can only get off the bus at the stop outside the school; that's where I have been trained to get off but all the other kids get off early and jog to school. I'd find that hard because there are lots of roads they cross. They would help me but at the same time they are in a rush, because they are going to be late for school, so they have to jog – some people do ask me to jog with them but I say, 'I think it will be safer not to'.

Year 9 pupil

Even though pupils with visual disabilities are technically fully included there are still aspects of school life from which they may be excluded, resulting in a significant absence of social knowledge and opportunities to develop friendships.

The social challenge: what we can do about it

The big picture: environmental audit

Environmental awareness and friendly helpfulness are important aspects of daily life at school for pupils with visual disabilities. Pupils need to know where things are and how they can find them safely and quickly so that they can participate more fully in all aspects of school life. A careful audit of the school environment can establish where straightforward adaptations may be made and also identify where dangers exist so that action can be taken to minimise or eliminate them altogether.

The Special Educational Needs and Disability Act

This Act came into force in September 2005 and gave pupils with disabilities new rights in mainstream schools. There is now a duty for all schools to plan to increase their accessibility over time and prepare an Accessibility Plan. The plan must have three strands:

▸ to increase access to the curriculum for pupils with a disability, e.g. teaching and learning arrangements, deployment of staff, timetabling and staff training;

▸ to improve access to written information for pupils with a disability and ensure that every pupil has access to all the information that is available to their peers, e.g. signage, hand-outs, textbooks, display, newsletters, information about school trips;

▸ to increase physical accessibility to all areas of the school.

All pupils need to be feel confident, not only in the classroom, but also in the wider school environment. Many pupils, not only those with visual disabilities, can be overwhelmed by the sheer size of a large school building and experience the environment as intimidating (Measor and Woods, 1984). Environmental factors therefore need to be considered not only in terms of ensuring safety and minimising hazards but positively ensuring the school building actually supports pupils' orientation by providing stable reference points and giving all pupils a secure sense of location and direction. The Royal Institute of British Architects (RIBA, 1981) provides a classic and straightforward six-point plan to maximise environmental safety and efficiency. These recommendations range from fundamental principles to be incorporated in the building at the design and planning stage to clear and specific guidelines for décor, illumination and room arrangement which can be used to inform Accessibility Plans:

▸ Orientation and simplicity of layout.

▸ Good lighting and elimination of glare.

▸ Use of colour and tone contrast.

▸ Use of texture contrast and tactile clues.

▸ Good acoustic conditions.

▸ Clear, large graphics at eye level.

An accessible school environment which enables pupils to participate fully in the life of the school is vital given that visual disabilities can be such a barrier to social development and participation.

Relationships are what matter most

The development of social competence is susceptible to the impact of a visual impairment (Warren, 1994). Reduced vision means that pupils are unlikely to be able to detect facial expressions, read body language correctly, make eye contact or detect a smile. It is not surprising therefore that many individuals with visual impairment have been described in terms of low self-esteem, passivity or limited assertiveness (Harrell and Strauss, 1986). The development of children with visual disabilities is best understood in terms of the social environment in which they find themselves and the quality of interpersonal encounters that arise within it. One important factor is the child's own ability to understand the social behaviour of others, to read social contexts and behave in a way that promotes acceptance.

Mainstream pupils have been described as the 'self-appointed gate keepers of inclusion' (Allan, 1999, p. 111) as they can by their attitude and behaviour promote either the inclusion or exclusion of pupils with disabilities. Pupils with visual disabilities may interact less frequently with their peers than their sighted classmates and therefore a systematic approach to promoting social interactions and friendships needs to be established within the school. Cooper et al. (1994) write that the institutional arrangements within a school have a profound effect on the social and emotional adjustment of their students and that schools have it in their power to inhibit or exacerbate the development of emotional and behavioural difficulties and also the capacity to operate as therapeutic agents.

Peer support programmes

The benefits of peer support programmes are summarised by Cowie and Wallace (2000) who suggest that they benefit children who have family and social problems, improve the general climate of the school and give social skills training to the peer supporters themselves. One of the best known peer support programmes, Circle of Friends (Pearpoint et al., 1992), is described by Stephen Dedridge in Chapter 2. However, for many pupils with visual disabilities who need to develop a strong self-concept and more assertive behaviours, developing a support network around the pupil may encourage passivity and a programme which targets a group of pupils may be more appropriate. *Teaching Peer Support for Caring and Co-operation: Talk Time* (MacConville and Rae, 2006) employs the basic framework of 'Circle of Friends' but targets a wider number of pupils and avoids what can sometimes be a difficulty with 'Circle of Friends' – that is, the focus on an individual pupil, and the inevitable discussion about the target pupil in their absence (Newton et al., 1996). This is not acceptable to some pupils (or staff) and may heighten the focus pupil's social isolation. Talk Time overcomes these difficulties by targeting a group of pupils who meet together weekly for approximately ten weeks to offer mutual support to each other. Unlike Circle of Friends, pupils do not volunteer to join the group but are carefully selected for the programme. The Talk Time group includes pupils who have high social status and others who may have low social status within the peer group.

Just as Circle of Friends emphasises that relationships are what matter most this programme also emphasises the importance of relationships. Pupils are encouraged to find and build on a shared sense of values and worth. The aim is to encourage the group members to talk to each other and make that conversation into one that develops over time and is increasingly shared with others in order to promote social growth within the school community. The focus throughout the programme is on developing language as a tool for thinking collectively and for co-reasoning. The group becomes the area of common ground between the selected pupils which is built up during each of the meetings. The more values and strategies are shared, the more a sense of community develops. What holds the intervention together is a structured way of doing things; the weekly meetings have a set routine: an introduction, setting and reviewing goals and focusing on positive solutions to the day-to-day practical problems that the pupils may encounter. By giving pupils the skills and support to handle low level incidents, peer support programmes mean that pupils become less reliant on staff for solving their problems. Sharing problems is a powerful way of letting pupils with visual disabilities know that they are not alone in experiencing difficulties in school.

> *He [English teacher] has this funny writing. He squishes the letters and words together. I go right up to the board and say, 'What's this?' Everyone's shouting, 'Get out my way, I can't see'. I say 'Neither can I.' I'm up at the board and I still can't read it. It's annoying and he [teacher] keeps saying I'm making fun of how he writes. I'm not. It's so annoying when I can't read the board.*
>
> *Year 8 pupil (sighted)*

The gap between what pupils can do on their own and what they can achieve with others more skilled than themselves is known as the 'zone of proximal development' (Vygotsky, 1978). Pupils with disabilities tend to have fewer opportunities to develop the skills that are generated by social interaction such as conflict, collaboration, competition with their peers and encounters with adults. Membership of a peer support group can redress this balance. Through social interaction with their more socially mature peers pupils are exposed to practices and ways in which others sort out their problems and manage their thinking. Providing the pupil who has visual disabilities with opportunities to meet with their peers in structured groups can be a valuable way of building the social confidence and self-esteem of all involved.

Support groups

If there are several pupils with visual disabilities in a school, meeting regularly as a group and sharing experiences can be a valuable way of providing opportunities for pupils to deal collaboratively with the specific issues that arise for them. Visual impairment is a low incidence disability; therefore a pupil may not have met another person with a visual disability or anyone who has been through what they have been experienced until they start high school. Children understand children and also take the time to listen to each other (Tyrell, 2002) and a group can provide an opportunity for pupils to provide support and encouragement for each other.

Terminology

Families and the pupils themselves may not have a vocabulary for their visual disability or for its effects or treatment. This can easily lead to a taboo in talking about the disability and leave pupils unable to answer questions about their disability and reluctant to talk to anybody including their family about their concerns. Pupils benefit from opportunities to consider a variety of words and phrases to describe their disability. When they are ready they can then choose how to describe themselves. It is important to encourage pupils to notice when terminology disturbs or seems unhelpful or wrong. Pupils tell us that being described as 'partially sighted' or 'blind' is far preferable to being called 'disabled'.

I would rather be called the whole thing – Visually Impaired Person – just not disability. It's a silly word. I don't like that word. There's hundreds and thousands of disabilities, and yes, 'Visually Impaired Person' is better than 'blind'. If people see 'disabled', they first think no brains and then they think no legs.

Year 8 pupil

If no one ever talks to a child about their visual disability, then they will have no starting place for dealing with the other's interest in it or their own sense of feeling different. Working with pupils on understanding their visual disability and practising appropriate responses to inevitable questions about it from others is an important step in the process of building confidence and promoting a positive sociable outlook.

Social skills

The safe context of a support group is also an appropriate place to develop more appropriate non-verbal language and address the development of the specific social skills which can be difficult for pupils with visual disabilities to acquire. Pupils may need to be taught the impact of verbal and non-verbal messages and how their passivity may affect others. These may include understanding the importance of looking towards the speaker during conversations and consciously developing a positive voice tone. Specific advice and coaching around social skills and strategies for managing uncomfortable feelings can lead to gains in social confidence and with such an understanding pupils will have more options from which to choose as they interact with others.

The learning environment: what young people tell us

The most frequent problem reported by pupils with visual disabilities in the classroom is difficulty with board work.

Seeing the board is really a problem for me in all lessons. I put my hand up and tell the teacher I can't see the board and they say do you want me to write it down on a piece of paper and then they forget.

Year 7 pupil

Teachers, they copy things up on the board which I can't see and I ask them if they can copy it and they say, 'No, just leave it, you won't need it' and then the next lesson I do need it.

Year 8 pupil

The board's a problem. In almost all lessons I'm expected to copy from the board. Sometimes in just one or two lessons I get a copy [of the work on the board] but in most lessons I don't and I just sit there – or I copy from a friend.

Year 8 pupil

Pupils tell us that they are extremely selective about the teachers whom they approach for help and report that most of the time they would rather go without the information and remain silent rather than draw attention to themselves. Even when pupils feel confident enough to ask for help they report that they are sometimes met with rebuffs:

I tell the teacher I can't read the board but he doesn't pay any attention. He just says, 'Oh go and sit down' or he says, 'Yes' but walks off to do something else.

Year 8 pupil

For many pupils the solution to not being able to see the board is to rely on a teaching assistant (TA) to act as a scribe.

Support is when you get somebody who comes and sits next to you and copies stuff off the board for you.

Year 7 pupil

The second most common problem that pupils report they experience in the classroom is the lack of enlarged texts. Pupils report that enlarged texts are often not available for them and report that they often have to wait while teaching assistants leave the classroom and get enlarged copies of texts or worksheets.

Teaching assistants (TAs)

The previous section highlighted the social difficulties faced by pupils in settings such as the playground or canteen. These are the obvious places where friendships can develop and although they may develop in the classroom they are less likely to do so. The frequency of the pupils' references to the 'friendship' provided by the TA in discussions about the classroom suggests that pupils rely on them for 'emotional holding' (Greenhalg, 1994) as much as for practical support such as scribing board work or providing enlarged copies of texts.

Yes, it makes me safe having him [TA] there and he copies things down from the board. I can't talk to teachers as much as I can to Mr S. I feel left out a bit without Mr S. I can talk about cars, football, anything to him, just as I am doing my work and all that. It doesn't disturb me because we don't speak that much – he's more friendly [than the teachers].

Year 8 pupil

*Mr S., my support person, he's cool and all the kids look up to him and the[...]
me for it because they know it's because of me he's there [in the classroo[...]
think that it's good having him in the classroom.*

Yea[...]

Pupils tell us that the support of a TA to scribe board work or provide enlarged copies of worksheets is usually preferable to acknowledging their disability by using specialist equipment such as binoculars, magnifiers and even spectacles in the classroom. Staff are often very unsure of how much a pupil can actually see and what tasks they are able to carry out independently and are therefore more likely to take at face value the pupil's request for help. Staff often do not appreciate that with sensitive encouragement and certain adaptations such as using binoculars, sitting at the front of the class, going up to the board, or asking the teacher to use a black rather than a coloured pen, some pupils are more likely to be able to access board work and texts for themselves. The presence of a TA, usually described by the pupils as 'support', can mean pupils do not have to openly acknowledge their disability and also brings the additional benefit of directly engaging with a member of staff.

Yes, I think it is easier to speak to your support person than your teacher because, well, it's easier to ask them things, they aren't as busy. I can also see them much better – they are up near to me. The teachers are far away. I can only see teachers if they come up near.

Year 8 pupil

For pupils with severe visual impairment and for those who are educationally blind, the amount of support they receive from a TA can be considerable and often equates to full-time assistance in the classroom. Although the preparation of teaching materials, photocopying, brailling materials, tactile maps, tables, charts, etc. is a main element of the TA's role a lack of time for planning and liaison with teachers can, as the following account by an experienced TA describes, leave pupil and TA stranded together in the classroom.

Sometimes when I'm in a classroom with Rickie the teacher begins to write on the board. She turns and says to the class, 'Now all look at this board. You can see what I've written, look at it carefully, read it and make notes on the information that you can see there.' Now he [Rickie] knows that I know that he can't see it. So he'll whisper to me, 'Oh yes, I'll look at the board, I'll read the information, no sweat'. I think that it is really good that we can make a joke of it. We have a good laugh about it together but quietly so nobody can hear or I'd get into trouble.

Pupils also report that a TA is often with them for most of the school day, often conducting a tutorial – 'a lesson within lesson' (Welding, 1996, p. 114) which is separate from the main body of the lesson. This parallel model of working is often at the detriment of social inclusion, and in practice means that pupils are taught exclusively by the TA if they are not able to access the information from the class teacher.

> *Well, Maths. Like she [maths teacher] does annoy me and I do crack jokes at her all day that she doesn't know about right. Like Miss [TA] and I just sit there and crack jokes at her [maths teacher] like because she says 'Can you see the board because I've put numbers on it so you can see it?' All this time other people have been working out what will help me see and it's just putting numbers in front of it that will make me see! Thing is she always writes on the board; she can't do anything but write on the board.*

> *Year 9 pupil*

A lack of communication between members of staff can cause pupils considerable frustration. Staff need to ensure that there is a team approach to including pupils and a consistent way of doing things.

> *Yes, I had problems with Mr G. [science teacher] in Year 8 'cos even though I had notes in my [homework] planner from Miss A. [SENCO] and Miss M. [TA] to let me go [out of class] and enlarge my work, he wouldn't accept that I was allowed to go out of the room. So I had some pretty rubbish times and he didn't explain things properly either, which made it really hard.*

> *Year 9 pupil*

> *If you're late you get detention. Miss B. [TA] told me I don't have to go. So I didn't go. Mr P. [form tutor] asked me why I didn't go to the detention. I explained to him Miss B. told me I didn't have to go and he says, 'Oh that's a nice set up!' I don't know what I felt like doing; I felt like beating him up!*

> *Year 8 pupil*

Pupils report, however, that as they gradually become more secure in the classroom, the continuous presence of a TA can become restrictive.

> *Don't tell Miss [TA] I told you this right, but it's bad having somebody breathing down your neck all day. Every two seconds it's, 'Listen to what the teacher is saying'. You are not allowed to speak to your friend or anything.*

> *And when Miss was away, the good stuff was that I could actually talk [in class] and do stuff. When Miss is with me it's not that I'm not allowed; it's just that it's hard to talk to my friends. If she's not with me, I can muck about. It's true. Do you want a stick over you all the time ready to tell you when you are doing something wrong?*

> *Year 9 pupil*

> *Yes, even I get frustrated by Miss [TA] when I'm with my mate.*

> *Year 9 pupil*

This sense of frustration caused by a lack of independence in the classroom is expressed very powerfully in the following poem written by a Year 10 pupil.

Blessing

The humans are stiffened like a statue
There is never enough movement.

Imagine being in a classroom
on your own without being assisted.
Just you, the students and a teacher.
Just for a single lesson,
the pleasure of slight freedom.

Sometimes I have a lesson
where I can be independent.
The joy and pleasure excites me,
it is a lucky day.
A smile appears on my face.
It lights up a room like illuminous paper.
It is impossible to miss.

The lesson continues.
I succeed on my own.
I am in control of my life,
I am not a stiff statue anymore,
I have been blessed.
I am being me.

Pupils tell us that the real taboo, however, is for the TA to get involved in their friendships:

> *Oh yes, Miss [TA] – you really embarrassed me this morning. Right in front of her [girl pupil] you said [to me], 'You ain't going to get a girlfriend by being sarcastic'. I was only having a joke with her and she goes to you, 'Can you read Braille?' So I said, 'No, she [TA] just pretends to'. I was joking with her because you [TA] really embarrassed me.*
>
> *Year 11 pupil*

Managing day-to-day routines

The presence of a visual disability means that the world is experienced in a fragmentary way. It is harder for children to establish concepts without the myriad of information that is received through clear and accurate vision. This is illustrated very starkly by the following example given by an experienced TA who had been working with pupils with visual disabilities for several years:

> *I mean he [Year 11 pupil with visual disability] asked me a question in a lesson and I said, 'I can't talk now'. He said a few minutes later, 'Have cars got certain shapes to them?' Then later when we was in the gym and they [the class] had basketball and he doesn't like basketball and he can't cope, so I take him into the gym and*

he's on the Multigym, the treadmill, and he goes, 'Miss, about these cars – do they have different shapes?' And I said 'Yes, why are you asking me?' And he said 'cos I was on the bus and Shane [peer] knew every car that went pass' – I said, 'But cars, they've got names on them and emblems – badges.' 'Oh have they? I was wondering how come he [Shane] knows.'

Fatigue

We also learn from listening to pupils that far more effort is needed to manage the business of day-to-day routines causing them stress and fatigue. It is generally understood that pupils with a visual disability get far more tired in school than their sighted peers (Arter *et al.*, 1999). Often the tiredness is directly related to the pupil's eye conditions. For pupils who have photophobia, the glare caused by sunlight can cause discomfort and tiredness which can lead to intense headaches.

> *When I go to high school I want the teachers to believe me when I say I have got a headache. I need them to know I am not making it up.*
>
> *Year 6 pupil*

We also learn from listening to pupils that far more effort is needed to manage the business of day-to-day routines, causing them stress. Pupils report that it takes them much longer to read texts and complete written work and that it often can be difficult and time consuming to read their own handwriting. Surviving in school, then, entails taking far more time over tasks, including homework, than their sighted peers.

> *Yesterday it took me ages to do my Science [homework] but I done it. It was a diagram of the rock cycle. All the different stages. I had to label them. I was using felt tips. I could see it [the diagram] – just – I was just about able to do it. It took me hours. Then I was so tired I went to sleep.*
>
> *Year 8 pupil*

The presence of a visual disability also means that it is difficult and time consuming for pupils to scan their surroundings and they report that they are therefore constantly checking for their belongings. The most critical items that pupils report that they lose track of are phones, glasses, keys and money.

> *I lost my phone and my glasses. It's the third time. It was a low [time]. My glasses and mobile were missing after the lesson. I went home and my dad went mad. I went to turn on the phone after the lesson and it was gone – someone's probably got it. The hospital won't give me another pair of glasses I've lost so many. My mum has to buy me glasses now.*
>
> *Year 7 pupil*

I lose money ... depends on what colour the floor is. If I drop it, I've lost it. It all blends in for me. When they give me change I can't see the colour of the notes to check it.

Year 7 pupil

The importance of listening

Pupils with visual disabilities tell us that listening is an important way in which they understand and engage with the world around them. Many blind and partially sighted people acknowledge the central role that hearing plays in their life (Goldstein, 1999).

I didn't want to go into the room. I didn't know who was there. I have to make them talk to know who's there. You must make them talk. I have to say something like, 'What do you think of this subject?'

Year 11 pupil

Even when pupils know who is present in a room, the difficulties that they experience in interpreting facial expressions and language mean that they rely on auditory clues to detect feelings and underlying messages.

In class it can be difficult knowing who is talking – you can get used to a teacher's voice and know who it is after a few weeks but it's harder in class to work out who else is talking. You can't exactly get your binoculars out to see who is there can you? If it's a big group, so many people (i.e. pupils) are talking you just rely on the voices to recognise who's talking. The classroom is OK because most of the time the teacher is the only one talking, but if there is group discussion, I just listen for voices. I think I nearly know everybody now by their voices.

Year 9 pupil

The teacher's voice and use of vocabulary are particularly valuable in motivating the pupil with a visual disability.

You cannot not listen to a PE teacher.

Year 11 pupil

Pupils tell us that an audible and interesting voice is essential to avoid the frustration that can occur if visual stimuli are reduced or absent.

I couldn't hear what he [headmaster] was saying. I was sitting at the back [of the hall] with the Year 10s and I really wanted to hear what happened to Charlie [a pupil who had died]. He [headmaster] was speaking so quietly. Everybody was listening. The hall was so big. I couldn't hear him so I didn't know what happened to Charlie. I had to wait until I saw Miss B. [TA] afterwards. She told me what he said.

Year 10 pupil

The learning environment: what we can do about it

Knowledge of the disability

It is generally accepted that the willingness of mainstream staff to understand the effects of the disability and also the challenges facing pupils with visual impairment is a key factor in successfully meeting their needs. So what does the class teacher or form tutor need to do differently in order to include a pupil with a visual impairment? First, it is essential that staff understand the pupil's eye condition and find out as much as possible about its practical implications for the classroom. A key role of the peripatetic (visiting) specialist teacher is to provide staff with this information. It was clear from the discussions with pupils that their own confidence in dealing with their visual disability is enhanced by the teacher's knowledge of the condition and willingness to adapt the work. Hence in a lesson where the teacher does not appear to be aware of the disability, the pupil is more likely to conceal it; an assertive and confident approach on the part of the staff member, however, encourages an assertive approach by the pupil.

> I don't mind [others knowing I'm visually impaired] in PE. This week the PE teacher, because he knows I'm partially sighted and can't see the high jump rope, put thick black foam around the rope so I could see it. Everybody knew he did that so I could see. I didn't mind because I could join in.
>
> *Year 10 pupil*

Talking to the pupil

Secondly, involving the pupils themselves in a dialogue about their visual disability is vital because as soon as a pupil is known to have a visual disability it sets up certain reactions. The most obvious is that people tend to notice the disability rather than the pupil and the label 'visual impairment' becomes viewed as the defining characteristic of the pupil. Labels tend to trigger generalisations so consequently all pupils with visual impairment will be viewed as having similar difficulties. In the case of visual impairment this is particularly a problem as it is a low incidence disability and generalisations will usually be based on limited experience. Pupils with apparently similar visual conditions and recorded levels of visual acuity may in fact have very different needs. The effects of visual disability are influenced by a range of factors which include the eye condition, age of onset of the eye condition, parental and family attitudes, but most importantly by the motivation, personality and social and emotional intelligence of the individual pupil. Gathering information from a variety of sources and listening carefully to the pupil until a picture begins to emerge takes time and patience.

Simply knowing that a pupil is visually impaired in fact tells us very little about what the pupil can see. An understanding of what a visual disability is like relies on having a dialogue with the child because the effects of the disability have such varied effects upon sight and create a range of problems. It is important that staff take steps to let the pupil know that they are aware of the pupil's difficulties and ensure that positive steps are taken to include the pupil.

Team work

The effective inclusion of pupils with disabilities requires a variety of professionals to work collaboratively together (Davis and Hopwood, 2002). Different professionals have different roles and responsibilities and the class teacher or form tutor plays an important role in bringing the various professionals together and will need to sort out ways of working as a team. Within the school setting these professionals will include the SENCO, TA and the specialist teacher of the visually impaired. Arrangements and targets for the pupil need to be agreed collaboratively in open meetings where everyone's perspective, including parents' and pupils', is valued. The team need to reach agreement on the important issues that affect the pupil's inclusion to avoid the pupil being subjected to contradictory demands and standards. Key instructional and environmental strategies which the team need to agree on to enable pupils with visual disabilities to become accepted and active participants in the classroom include preferential seating arrangements and a classroom environment that respects all members and their contributions. A significant number of pupils who were interviewed commented on how the work of a TA had influenced their behaviour and feelings about school; it follows therefore that a TA who does not feel included in the team is unlikely to be able to effectively support the pupil's inclusion in the school. Pupils do best and are happier when professional teams are harmonious, communicative, sensitive and imaginative to each other and to the child's needs and keep the pupil's participation in and enjoyment of school activities, both academic and social, as the main focus.

Not enough information

It has been estimated that approximately 80 per cent of what we know about the world has been learnt through sight (Mehrabian,1972). It is important for staff to be aware that pupils with visual disabilities may not always have a similar level of general information as their sighted peers. It is sometimes difficult for staff to appreciate the gaps in their knowledge as pupils are characteristically at pains to appear 'normal' and not stand out as being different. Also as pupils become more familiar with their surroundings their difficulties become increasingly camouflaged. Put the pupil in a less familiar environment, however, and difficulties are likely to become far more apparent.

Staff need to be aware that everyday experiences may not provide pupils with the type of information that comes by chance in an unstructured, 'untaught', spontaneous way to sighted pupils. Tobin (1998) illustrates this by citing the example of Diana who at age 14 (and who subsequently went on to take a university degree) did not understand that if jars containing sand or plasticine were put into a bucket of water there would be a rise in the level of water. Diana said, 'No, nothing happens when the jars are put in the bucket' (p. 110). Diana did not seem to understand that the level of water would change at all. Tobin writes that he did not believe that the task was beyond Diana and persevered with different examples until at last she recognised that if she stepped into a bath filled to the brim with water, some of it would spill over and be displaced, at which point 'She laughed aloud' (p. 110). Tobin suggests that there are particular learning and other contexts where the absence of vision prevents the acquisition of information that serves to:

▸ provide a synoptic overview;

▸ highlight what is most important;

▸ allow immediate confirmation or correction.

Multi-sensory approach

Children with visual disabilities may frequently experience bewilderment and misunderstanding. Conjecture based on what may be wrong information will create further misunderstanding. Millar (1994) writes that completeness and assurance is the result of information that comes through multi-sensory (sight, hearing, touch) channels and is overlapping and complementary. It is therefore important to provide pupils with sufficient opportunities to learn by doing, in the context of supportive relationships so that the pupil will have the confidence to ask meaningful questions. To the child with a visual disability, questioning is a form of orientating and checking what is going on. Answers are vital. If questions go unanswered or if the situation is such that the child does not feel able to ask questions, then the pupil will continue to experience misinformation. In this context staff need to always take fear and distress extremely seriously.

Effective communication

Pupils with a visual disability have a tendency to be quiet (Corley *et al.*, 1989) and have to be taught to be effective verbal communicators of their own inner states. The language lag observed in many pre-school children with visual disabilities (Dunlea, 1989) does not just disappear. Pupils have to learn to have the confidence to speak their mind and assert their presence through talking as the non-verbal skills of making eye contact, 'reading' body language, recognising their peers may not be available to them. Pupils require additional adult help and explanation at an age when many of their peers have usually acquired a wide vocabulary and sophisticated concepts. This is often difficult to achieve in a large group of children because although children talking to each other can undoubtedly enhance verbal skills, for the pupil with a visual disability this will not be enough and lack of communication can contribute to the persistence of false ideas and misconceptions. Two adults in the classroom can be very advantageous as the increased staff ratio can be targeted to ensure that the pupil can be part of conversations and also that specific issues such as the failure to repair messages during breakdowns in communication and the misinterpretation of behaviour or intent can be addressed. The need for staff to encourage pupils with visual disabilities to communicate and express themselves is not always emphasised and often support is used exclusively for practical activities such as learning routes, avoiding physical hazards, copying information from the board and enlarging texts.

Good listening

Environmental sounds are a crucial source of information enabling us to tune in to what is happening around us. Contrary to popular belief, however, visual disability does not automatically lead to the development of sophisticated listening skills (Miller and Ockelford, 2005). The auditory environment needs to be rich in order to fill in the information which is not quickly available by use of the eyes. Making use of sound information is not possible if the environment is either too noisy or too quiet. It is important that pupils with visual disabilities are taught in classrooms which are not constantly invaded by unwanted sounds as they need to be encouraged to detect significant sounds and ignore superfluous noise.

The situation is not as simple as that, as hearing replaces vision as a source of information about what is going on. The effective decoding of others' facial expressions assists in the understanding of emotions and in producing a more accurate understanding of the social situation as a whole. The lack of ability to fully access non-verbal cues puts pupils with visual disabilities at risk; the look, the smile, the glare, the raised eyebrow, a theatrical silence or the closing of a book are 'lost' on them. Much feeling is carried in the voice and it is important to realise that if pupils have difficulty interpreting facial expressions and body language, they are likely to rely heavily on clues from the voice concerning feelings, emotions and the underlying message. Voice management is a critical element of successful teaching.

Not enough time

Pupils with visual disabilities take longer to process information than their peers. They have to work far harder and for much longer to reach the same standard and therefore they tend to get very tired in school (Tobin, 1998). At all stages of the education system information is presented in visual form (printed texts, graphs, maps and pictures) which has to be processed quickly. Staff need to recognise that it will take the pupil with a visual disability much longer to read texts and complete written work. They may also find it difficult and time consuming to read their own handwriting. Many of these difficulties can be addressed by, for example, the provision of IT equipment, touch-typing skills, access to enlarged materials and the provision of additional time to complete tasks. The pupils themselves must also be encouraged to positively manage their tiredness by getting more rest and having a nutritious diet. Many of the pupils I interviewed appeared to be unaware that there was a connection between the extreme levels of tiredness that they frequently experienced in school and their visual disability.

Low vision aids (LVAs)

Pupils tell us that what is most important to them in school is to appear 'normal'. Although using LVAs such as magnifiers and binoculars may significantly improve what they can see, pupils often tell us that they are reluctant to use them as the social price of standing out from their peers and looking different is too high. Pupils are not helped by being criticised, warned or punished for not using specialist equipment. They do better when instances of compliance are recognised with quiet appreciation for the discomfort that the pupil is willing to tolerate. The introduction of equipment at an early age and the opportunity to get used to it at home can be effective in encouraging its use. The willingness to use special equipment varies greatly from pupil to pupil and what is acceptable to one pupil may be rejected by another. Pupils report that they need to find their own threshold of what is acceptable and that just because they are willing to use one LVA does not mean they will accept another piece of equipment.

> *I've got a [white] cane; that's fine but I don't want a guide dog. I don't need one. I don't mind having a real dog – you know what I mean – I don't mind having a dog which is not a guide dog so anybody can get one. You don't train a dog and give it to someone who doesn't need it, do you? They won't even sell one [guide dog] to you; they think, what is the point?*
>
> *Year 11 pupil*

Where there are concerns or queries about the use of equipment it is vital that school, home and the medical team work together to ensure the pupil is not subject to contradictory or unrealistic demands.

Information technology (IT)

The introduction of computers, interactive whiteboards and sound field systems into schools has made the use of IT equipment in classrooms usual practice. One positive approach to the acceptance of special equipment is to explain its use to the whole class and let pupils use it so that it is relevant to everybody. The skilful use of a piece of interesting technology by a pupil with a visual disability can become a source of pride rather than embarrassment.

Interactive whiteboards

Interactive whiteboards have been particularly useful for enhancing the inclusion of pupils with visual disabilities. This equipment, if used in conjunction with blinds in the classroom to ensure that there is maximum contrast and coupled with increased font size, can mean that many pupils can read the board if they are sitting towards the front of the classroom. Alternatively pupils may prefer to access information directly from the teacher's monitor. If the monitor is not accessible, then cabling from the projector to a second monitor located in the pupil's work station may be a solution. If the teacher is using a pre-prepared presentation, for example on PowerPoint, this can be printed off before the lesson so the pupil has a personal copy of the text. Information can also be scanned from the interactive whiteboard in order to provide pupils with personal copies of the text.

Conclusion

This chapter has described the key themes that arise in pupils' accounts of being included in mainstream schools. The evidence they present paints a complex and multi-layered picture. It tells us about the diversity of their experiences and the danger of making sweeping generalisations about their need for specialist services and equipment. Each pupil faces unique challenges so that it is essential that strategies are negotiated with each individual rather than assuming an approach will work. Children have the potential to achieve much more if we listen to them and treat what they say seriously. Although the views of pupils who were included in this chapter show that uncomfortable experiences and strained relationships do exist, overall pupils emphasise that they value their mainstream placement and are 'actively seeking inclusion'. One of the important messages of this chapter, therefore, is the need to attend to and respect the views of pupils and their ability to 'tell it like it is'. When pupils have an effective voice, services can be delivered more effectively.

Useful websites

www.rnib.org.uk

www.nbcs.org.uk

www.clearvisionproject.org

www.nlbuk.org

www.revealweb.org.uk

www.calibre.org.uk

Chapter 4

Including Pupils with Specific Learning Difficulties

Dr Ruth M. MacConville
Stephen Dedridge
Ann Gyulai

Introduction

Specific learning difficulties usually referred to as SpLD, is a generic term which covers a range of different types of learning difficulties. A pupil may have difficulties with physical co-ordination and be identified as dyspraxic or have difficulties with numbers and be termed dyscalculic. Dyslexia is the most common type of SpLD identified at present; however, many prefer to use the term SpLD. Reid (2005) suggests that reluctance to use the term 'dyslexia' can be traced back to the Warnock Report (DES, 1978) which sought to remove from schools the previously rigid and harmful categorisations of learning difficulties. The Warnock Report acknowledged the presence of children who had unexpected and unusual difficulties in literacy, but emphasised that the term 'dyslexia' was not helpful to describe this population and recommended that the term 'specific learning difficulties' was more appropriate. Reid (2005) writes that education authorities were subsequently reluctant to use the term 'dyslexia'. Although the term dyslexia is increasingly recognised in schools and in government and professional publications it is still highly controversial.

The word dyslexia originates from the Greek (*dys* = impaired and *lexia* = word) and when translated into contemporary English means 'difficulty with words or language'. While this is an extremely simplistic definition it provides an insight into the challenges in reading, writing, spelling and in expressing thoughts on paper experienced by many individuals. During the past decade, the concept of dyslexia has developed and moved away from a discrepancy view between general ability and literacy skills to one which considers literacy sub-skills or cognitive building blocks that facilitate our ability to read, write and spell. The outcome of broadening the perception of dyslexia to include sub-skills has resulted in more individuals being identified as dyslexic. According to the British Dyslexia Association (BDA) around 4% of the population are severely dyslexic and a further 6% have mild to moderate problems.

The increase of the use of the term 'dyslexia' has reignited a longstanding and at times fierce debate and to account for the increasingly wide range of difficulties associated with dyslexia numerous definitions and theories have been developed, each with a particular focus. Explanations, assessment and treatment of dyslexia resemble the poem of the 'Six Blind Men and the Elephant' (traditional tale). In the poem each blind man catches hold of one bit of the animal – the trunk or the leg or the tail – and on the basis of this works out his own theory of what an elephant looks like. Different professionals look at dyslexia from different perspectives, often blinded to the views emanating from other disciplines and in doing so often fail to grasp dyslexia in its entirety. Perhaps more words have been written about dyslexia than about almost any other learning disability and practitioners working with this population have been confused by a myriad of different models and theories from which teaching materials have been developed often without being sufficiently tried and tested (Reid, 2005).

Over a decade ago Stanovitch (1994) neatly summarised the situation when he wrote that 'the term dyslexia is out of favour ... [because] it carries with it so many empirically unverified connotations and assumptions that consequently many researchers and practitioners prefer to avoid the term' (p. 579). On 9 September 2005, the Channel 4 *Dispatches* programme entitled 'The Dyslexia Myth' was aired. The controversy that followed this programme and related media articles reignited the long fought debate about the existence of dyslexia. Professor Julian Elliott of Durham University, one of the academics at the centre of the storm, argued that despite all his experience as an educational psychologist he does not accept that among the broader group of struggling readers there is a special group of pupils with a different IQ who need special intervention to help them overcome their reading problems. Professor Elliott also emphasised not that dyslexia does not exist but that there are now simply too many dyslexic children to make the term 'dyslexia' meaningful. Maggie Snowling, Professor of Psychology at York University, retorted that 'dyslexia is not a myth' (TES, 2005). Snowling argued that non-dyslexics tend to do well on programmes such as 'Reading Intervention' (one of the eighteen programmes identified by a government sponsored evaluation of schemes for poorer readers, 'What Works for Children with Literacy Difficulties', by Professor Greg Brooks from Sheffield University) but that dyslexics fare badly with 26 per cent of pupils making no progress at all. Snowling emphasised that these are the children we should label as dyslexic and provide more intensive support for them. There are very few, however, who would argue that there is such a thing as a typical dyslexic and as Cassar et al. (2005) observe often difficulties that are seen as typical of dyslexics are similarly found in younger normal readers who read at the same level.

Whatever the definition used, at the core of a specific learning difficulty is a processing difficulty which can be auditory, visual or motor in nature, or a combination of these three, which hinders the acquisition of literacy skills. Working memory, which allows us to follow conversations or stories and extract the salient points, may also be impacted. A reduced working memory can adversely affect an individual's ability to make sense of what they hear or read, or recall of information. It is of course important to emphasise that not all individuals will experience all three types of processing difficulties or a significantly reduced working memory function. The term specific learning difficulties rather than dyslexia will be used in most instances throughout this chapter in line with Reid's (2005) observation that the term SpLD is preferred by practitioners because many children and young people have difficulties which overlap with more than one category or have specific learning difficulties that do not fit the usual categories.

Personal account

Hassan

My name is Hassan and I'm 17 years old. I'm doing Drama and Sociology A levels.

When I went to school, at first I really enjoyed it but then it felt like everybody else in the class could read and write and I couldn't. It was trying really hard but my teacher wasn't very helpful and she just used to call me lazy and say I needed to pay attention more.

My parents were not much better. My dad would spend ages trying to make me sound out letters from books. I would get it one moment and then forget it the next and he would get really angry with me.

I was taken out of lessons to work with this lady in the Special Needs room. I quite liked going to her but some of the other kids said I went to her because I was stupid. I started saying clever, cheeky things to the teacher in class because that made the other kids laugh and stop calling me names.

My reading got a bit better but I still couldn't spell and no one could read my handwriting. When I got told I was dyslexic that really helped me because it meant I wasn't stupid or lazy. My parents didn't get as angry with me and the teachers seemed more patient.

Now I just think of being dyslexic as who I am; it doesn't make me any better or any worse than anyone else – it is just who I am. I learnt to use a computer and type most of my work now which is really great as no one used to be able to read what I wrote. I used to destroy my work at primary school before anyone could see it because I hated my handwriting so much.

I used my computer in the GCSEs which really helped. I know I am still not cured of dyslexia. It still affects me. I have to make lists of everything. But then I lose the lists. And people tell me something and I straightaway forget it and they say, 'How can you forget it ? I just told you'. Sometimes I think my brain works too fast and is always buzzing even at night when I want to get to sleep. That is how I write. My teachers say I have lots of good ideas but they are all over the place.

I go to a drama school out of school and I want to be an actor. I could get my dad or my brother to read out my lines on a tape so I could learn them without reading them so I don't think that would be a problem – well reading, although I think I would have to work very hard to remember them.

The social challenge: what young people tell us

The emotional and cognitive sides of SpLD are permanently intertwined and literacy difficulties have serious implications for how pupils feel about themselves. Humphrey (2002) emphasises the importance of self-concept and self-esteem for factors such as motivation, academic achievement and peer relationships. We learn from listening to pupils that their levels of achievement strongly influence how they view themselves.

> *In Year 3 I thought I was clever, but they [teachers] said I was left behind and they put me down from group 2 to the lowest group so I just felt useless and lost interest in school. I didn't care anymore. I couldn't read, write or spell easily and that affected how I felt about myself. The worst effects of my reading and spelling problems are feeling stupid and not being able to write easily or properly and my work and homework take just ages.*
>
> *Year 8 pupil*

Isolation

Scott (2003) suggests that school is where problems start and where problems are perpetuated and that lowered levels of self-esteem spring directly from the attitudes and behaviour of other people. We are all defined through the behaviour and reactions of others and pupils tell us that when their literacy difficulties emerge in school they begin to be treated in a new and inexplicably uncomfortable way. A feeling expressed by some young people is that of isolation. Pupils often tell us that they believe that they are the only one in their class or even their school with their kind of difficulties and that there is no one to talk to who understands what they are going through.

Public failure

Pupils know instinctively from a very early age that of all school learning, nothing compares in importance with reading; it is of unparallel significance (Bettelheim and Zelan, 1982). Thus the experience of having a problem with reading can be devastating. The very public failure to learn to read and later write can soon lead to a sense of inadequacy or poor self-image.

> *I'm afraid no one will like me when they find out I can't spell.*
>
> *Year 4 pupil*

Sometimes either disruptive or withdrawn behaviour follows.

> *I take my son to school every day and he gets to the gates and just freezes and has a bad anxiety attack. Sometimes I manage to get him into the gates and leave*

him at reception. When I have to leave him he just totally panics and it seems it is only getting worse because the older he gets the stronger he gets and he becomes harder to handle for me. He has said that he wants to kill himself on many occasions due to his frustrations with not being able to read and write properly and his anger with school. He has never fitted in at any school he has gone to due to being bullied at his primary school and now at high school. I am at my wit's end. My son can't work in class as he says he feels very uncomfortable having people sitting around him criticising and making fun of his work, especially the children who began bullying him because of his reading difficulties. This has happened all through his school years from Reception to high school. He also finds loud noises a very hard issue to deal with, especially in the classroom. He also has co-ordination problems and very low self-esteem.

Parent of Year 7 pupil

At first pupils tell us that they cannot understand exactly what the problem is. They work as hard as other pupils but do not make similar progress. Young people tell us that they feel under constant pressure to keep up with the work and become anxious and frustrated as most of their classmates appear to 'sail through'. As they get older pupils become increasingly comparative with their peers and tell us that although they 'keep getting told off' or are told to 'hurry up' they know that they are already working much harder than their classmates and become increasingly reluctant to ask their peers for support.

There is no way I would ask anyone to help me. You just get the hidden message that you're stupid, they look at me in a funny way when I'm having a problem like I'm stupid and I also feel bad for my friends too because I know they hate it when they see me struggling and can't do anything to help. Writing down homework from the board was a nightmare for me – I always go home with it mostly all missing.

Year 8 pupil

Mixed messages

Despite all the effort that they pour into their work pupils tell us they are often told by adults that they are lazy and not making progress. Alternatively pupils report that people are very nice to them, often unnecessarily so, but despite the bright smiles and empty praise what they really hear are patronising undertones and the sub-text that something is wrong.

My main problem was my teacher's and my parents' attitude to me, which in time ended up completely crushing my self-esteem. I found it hard to keep going on with things. There was an intense fear of writing anything down, getting it on paper because of the panic of getting it wrong. There is no point stressing. I'm still a bad speller but I'm better than I was and I still dread writing anything down so I always use a computer and if I've got to write anything, I make myself do it right away so that I don't dread it and put off doing it.

Year 12 pupil

Including Pupils with Specific Learning Difficulties **71**

Sadly many pupils quickly reach the conclusion that they are 'worthless', 'rubbish', 'a pile of crap' because they read this in the voices, body language and sometimes direct statements of others.

> *I always had problems at school. I got angry, frustrated and I was teased. I always had to write a lot; there was never a place for a short bit of writing. We always had to write six pages so the teacher could get the marking done. All the things in school that got praise I couldn't do. It was the survival of the fittest, like a sausage factory with finest sausages at one end and economy sausages at the other. My work was always sub-standard and that made me feel sub-standard like an economy sausage.*
>
> *Year 11 pupil*

These personal recollections match the findings of Riddick's (1996) study. Riddick interviewed 22 children with literacy difficulties and reported that the pupils felt 'disappointed, frustrated, ashamed, fed up, sad, depressed, angry and embarrassed about their difficulties' (p. 129).

Young people tell us that they find it particularly distressing and humiliating when their difficulties are exposed to their classmates. Reading out loud in front of peers and getting the lowest mark in spelling tests are identified as particularly stressful. Pupils recall the fear they experience as their turn to read aloud approaches and describe the embarrassment as they stumble over the words, often missing the point of what they are reading. Their focus is on the struggle with reading rather than listening to the content of the readers who came before them.

> *Our English teacher in Year 7 would go through the register making each child read aloud to the rest of the class. As it got closer and closer to my name, it was like torture. I almost felt like running out of the class. By the time it came to me, I had lost my place in the book so the girl sitting next to me had to point to where I should start. Then I would try and sound out the words. The other kids would start to snigger. I would go bright red. The teacher would tell them off but in a way that just made it worse. After the lesson, some of the boys did impersonations of me trying to read. One of them told me I read like a spastic and ought to go to a special school. I started truanting off school. I have no idea why the teacher made me read aloud. I mean she knew I couldn't do it so what did it prove?*
>
> *Year 7 pupil*

The experience of public failure may be repeated dozens of times every day. Pupils confide in us that they sit in class dreading that they will be asked to read aloud. They tell us about the strategies they use to avoid being selected by the teacher so that their difficulties will not be exposed.

> *People in my class probably think I'm miserable because I keep my head down in class and try not to look at anybody. If Miss asks a question or anything I just look*

down at the desk. I really don't want to be asked to do anything in class; I know I'll just get it wrong.

Year 9 pupil

Practitioners know that if a pupil experiences significant difficulty with reading and writing they are usually at risk of getting left behind, not just during lessons but also in the playground. Public humiliation within the classroom is very closely linked to bullying in the playground. Pupils with literacy difficulties are often marked out socially as losers, stigmatised by other pupils and consequently seek other ways – from bullying to withdrawing from social interaction – to disguise their problem. Palmer (2006) writes that these children are often as intelligent as their classmates but they are operating on a tenth of their social power.

Peer attitudes

Peer attitudes can be a crucial factor in inhibiting or promoting access for pupils with disabilities (Rose and Shevlin, 2004). Pupils with learning difficulties, whether specific or general, are at increased risk of bullying and teasing and are less likely to be accepted by their peer group (Humphrey, 2002). Pupils describe the name calling which they are subject to at school. The most frequent and painful is 'thicko' and many pupils appear to have internalised the message that they are not 'normal'. Pupils often tell us that their lives would be much easier if people understood more about their difficulties.

Coping strategies

In order to avoid name calling from their peers and the disapproval of adults, many young people tell us that they spend time and energy hiding their difficulties. Some of these strategies can be thought of as 'positive' coping strategies but others are avoidance tactics which increase their long-term difficulties. Pupils tell us that they avoid using words in their writing which they cannot spell and, as often as they can, put off or avoid producing written work altogether. Pupils describe the dreadful inertia that they experience when they know that a piece of written work has to be completed and the procrastination they engage in order to do anything other than put pen to paper. Many young people tell us that they elect to produce work which is 'dumbed down' both in length and in vocabulary rather than writing what they want to say and face being accused of being careless or being 'punished' for making numerous spelling corrections.

This teaching assistant got me to copy out each spelling mistake I made ten times. It felt like I was been punished and I knew it wasn't helping me to learn the word. If I looked at a word and she covered it up, then I was able to spell it but a little while later I had forgotten how to spell the word again. This seemed to irritate her.

Year 10 pupil

Specific Learning Difficulties

One way I found of avoiding spelling mistakes was to just use more simple words –
so if I thought of the word 'worst', I would write 'bad', instead because I could spell
'bad', but I think that doing that all the time made my writing rubbish.

Year 10 pupil

Constant pressure

Another effect of 'being behind' is the constant pressure that pupils tell us
that they are put under by teachers and by parents to improve their literacy
skills:

In school my teacher expects me to spend every spare minute learning spellings
and then when I get home my mother thinks that me watching TV is a waste of
time. She would much rather see me struggling with a book.

Year 7 pupil

Pupils tell us that they are aware of the discrepancy between their 'real' (i.e.
cognitive and verbal) abilities and the literacy skills that they are able to
demonstrate in school:

The worst thing for me is the frustration, the sense that I am constantly
underperforming. Verbally I know I am much more astute and capable, I know I am
much more intelligent than my written work would suggest. I'm working hard but
seem to be getting nowhere. It's definitely not laziness.

Year 12 pupil

I'm confident to answer questions in class because I always know the answers and
I won't get it wrong but I still feel stupid because I can't read or write easily or
properly and doing my homework takes ages. Everybody knows that about me so
even though I know a lot and can explain things nobody takes me seriously.

Year 8 pupil

Hutchinson (2006) estimates that as many as 40 per cent of boys are turned
off literacy by the end of primary school and fail to achieve the average
level in writing which then leads them to require more teacher time as a
consequence of their disruptive behaviour. Many enter a vicious circle in
which their disaffection results in sanctions which in turn creates greater
resentment.

I get into trouble when I try to get help from the teacher who is helping someone
else. I automatically switch off. I turn to my friends, talk to them and start mucking
about and I get told off.

Year 9 pupil

Social behaviour

Shyness, lack of self-confidence or physical awkwardness can keep children and young people on the outskirts of social situations. Palmer (2006) suggests that 'the getting of literacy' (p. 201) creates enriched neural networks in children's brains which may be significant in the development of social behaviour. Pupils with SpLD also may have more difficulty fitting in because many social activities require quick thinking and verbal wit and pupils may not get the jokes or understand subtle verbal cues. Pupils tell us that by not wanting to look stupid they laugh when they don't understand the joke and then can usually tell by the look on the person's face that they have laughed before the punch line and totally missed the point. Pupils may also be cut off from the peer group because of their processing difficulties and problems with word recall and memory which on the surface appear to be immature social skills.

> *I keep saying 'what?' all the time because I don't understand what people say to me. I have to really think before I can make any sense of it and answer. It's worse if other people are talking at the same time. I can't concentrate on one voice and every little noise distracts me and then my mind goes foggy and I can't think straight.*
>
> *Year 8 pupil*

Problems with information processing also cause delay in understanding so during conversations pupils can still be working out what has just been said while for their peers the conversation has moved on and consequently the young person is left behind.

> *When people talk to me I hear them like they are blurry and scrambled. Words sometimes sound to me like they are on a radio when you are going through a tunnel; some are clear and some are fuzzy and no matter how much I concentrate it mostly all gets jumbled up.*
>
> *Year 8 pupil*

Pupils tell us that it is their inability to recall for a moment their best friend's name and describe the panic of knowing that at any moment 'mind blurriness' may kick in. Scott (2003) suggests the 'blank look that often accompanies the perusal of incoming data is off-putting. It can make a person seem uncommunicative or even slightly simple and discourages the rapid to-and-fro of chat which bonds a peer group' (p. 83). This can be devastating for the developing self (O'Moore, 2000).

Personal organisation

Scott (2003) emphasises that young people with specific literacy difficulties often have distinctive characteristics of their own: 'their information processing

Specific Learning Difficulties

delays, short-term memory deficit, irregular perceptions of time and sequencing can give an alarming spin to appointment keeping and communication' (p. 82). Pupils tell us that they experience problems with personal organisation and are often late, disorganised, lose or forget things and misread and misunderstand instructions. Anderson (1994) has described the school bags of pupils with specific literacy difficulties as 'looking like snowstorms in Chicago'.

> *I have a lot of problems getting myself together; I lose my homework, my desk is really messy and I don't know how to organise my desk, my bedroom or my locker so I am always losing things such as my jacket, trainers, my watch and even my packed lunch. So what I do is carry everything with me all the time so I've always got what I need for anything that happens. I can't properly plan ahead and so unless I have everything with me I'm usually in big trouble.*
>
> *Year 9 pupil*

Problems with sequencing and their perception of the concept of time can mean that pupils can fail to get to class on time and may get lost within a maze of corridors that all look the same. Memory problems may also result in lost work, forgotten deadlines, mislaid books and school bags. Pupils tell us that they like following timetables because they help them to know in advance what they are going to have to do and exactly where they need to go.

Staff attitudes

Elliott (2006 p. 36) writes 'some pupils get very demoralised because they have ability and yet people perceive them as idiots'. Many of these experiences involved their class teachers calling them stupid or lazy or both.

> *My teacher wasn't very helpful and she just used to say I was lazy and I didn't want to work.*
>
> *Year 7 pupil*

This is unacceptable because, as Pollock and Walker (1994) observe, if teachers tell pupils that they are stupid, lazy or slow, they will come to believe just that. Far from being lazy, pupils with SpLD use nearly five times more brain power than other children while performing language tasks (Frank and Livingston, 2003). Other pupils talked to us about members of staff who talked to them and 'treated them just like everybody else'. However, there was also more general experience of being patronised and a feeling that kindly patronisation, described by one pupil as the 'grandmother effect', is not conducive to either high academic expectations or positive relationships with staff.

> *Well, as far as I am concerned there was this definite culture of having to feel grateful for any help I got. A teacher would visit me in school and say to me, 'Do you know how*

lucky you are that I am here to visit you today? It costs a lot of money for me to be here with you today and you are very lucky to have been chosen to see me'. There was this general thing that basically they made you feel 'where would you be without us?' One day I was so annoyed and fed up with being made to feel guilty and I said, 'And what job would you have without us?'

Year 11 pupil

Reading and intelligence

Humphrey and Mullins (2002) emphasise that pupils with SpLD perceive a significantly stronger association between ability at reading and intelligence than other pupils and believe that being good at reading means you are intelligent. Elliott (2006) confirms there is still the assumption that to be a poor reader you must be 'thick' and writes that there is a widespread misconception that difficulties with reading and writing are linked to IQ:

> Reading isn't something that requires a high level of intelligence and amongst children who are struggling to read you find some with high IQ, some in the middle and some with a low IQ. The real tragedy of that misconception lies in the fact that children who are poor readers are too often assumed to be less capable: they are put into lower teaching groups, given easier work and are not intellectually challenged as they should be. (p. 37)

Pupils also tell us that because the emphasis in school is on academic results which depend on well-developed literacy skills, they feel that if they display their own particular strengths, they can be disregarded or even cause resentment:

> *If you read badly, write badly and sit quietly in a corner and draw, then that's OK but if you are articulate and challenging, or if you are clever and articulate but don't write well, then people don't like it, they can't work out what to do with you. But if you are bad at everything, then the teacher is more relaxed and just gets on with it.*

Year 11 pupil

Lower ability groups

Elliott (2006) observes that pupils are placed in lower ability groups on the basis of difficulties related to their literacy rather than their intellectual ability. Pupils tell us that they get placed in small groups with other pupils who cannot read and in that context often develop supportive allegiances with each other. Proximity is the antecedent of friendship so in the regular groupings pupils tell us that they build close allegiances with pupils who are much less able than themselves. Although the purpose of the small group is ostensibly to improve levels of literacy in fact pupils tell us that they are all too aware that the group contains pupils who, unlike themselves, need a great deal of help with understanding and come to rely on them to answer the questions, help with homework, build rapport with the teacher and generally mask the greater difficulties of their less able peers.

As Elliott (2006) concludes:

> You can have a really able child who is being given Mickey Mouse things to do by a teacher. Teachers need to look at whether the child's cognitive ability is somehow being underestimated, where children in the bottom set are given some type of worksheet (say missing words), but this child wants to learn about photosynthesis. What this means in effect is that they not only underachieve, they may also become disaffected and are unenthusiastic about learning. (p. 35)

The relief of diagnosis

The author Elisabeth Kübler-Ross (1969) in her classic work, talks about the five stages of the grieving process: denial, anger, bargaining, depression and acceptance – that occur when a loss such as a death, divorce or diagnosis of a disability occurs in the family. Moorehead's (2005) description of the time the official label arrives as a moment of triumph sums up the attitude of many pupils and their feelings that 'best of all the dyslexia test incorporates an IQ test, to prove to any doubters out there that you are not thick'.

> *I was diagnosed when I was in Year 2. I think I was glad when I was told that, because before that I had just thought I was stupid.*
>
> *Year 10 pupil*

Pupils report that teachers start looking at them in a different way. Many perceive the diagnosis of dyslexia to have both practical and social consequences but also a deeper significance. It provides a legitimate framework from which to understand their difficulties and the opportunity to receive practical help. But apart from the confirmation and relief that they are not 'thick', what exactly does being dyslexic mean to the pupils themselves?

> *It's something that [is] not working normal in my brain and it makes me get letters muddled up and it makes me forget things; it makes me not be able to get things in the proper order.*
>
> *Year 8 pupil*

Asked how he felt about being diagnosed this pupil answered, 'Not bothered', yet when asked if any of his peers ever made derogatory comments about him he answered, 'No, because I'd punch them', which would indicate that at some level he was affected by the negative association with the diagnostic label. Other pupils also offer a medicalised explanation for their difficulties:

Dyslexia? It's sort of like an ongoing illness or syndrome I've got. I think that as I'm growing up I've come to terms with what I've got, so it's easier for me now. I have learnt to live with it.

Year 12 pupil

Many pupils, however, are keen to assert their personal identity rather than accept a diagnosis. Such pupils resist association with what they perceive to be the stigma of a label and are committed to keeping a veil of secrecy over their diagnosis.

When she was first diagnosed, it was a relief, such a weight off my shoulders. I was telling people she had been diagnosed but she was furious with me: 'You haven't told them have you? I don't want them to know. Why did you tell them Mum? You knew I didn't want anybody to know.'

Parent of Year 6 pupil

For some pupils, believing that they had dyslexia internalised the idea that they were damaged and only very specialist teaching could mend or fix them. Many pupils, however, do not want to be regarded as different and for them there is a stigma associated with dyslexia which negatively impacts on their identity. For these pupils their attitudes to diagnosis can be complex and multi-layered.

I don't like having dyslexia. I can't stand the boring lessons outside the classroom – they make me not want to learn to read and I want to get by without reading. I want to be in class with my friends and not be different.

Year 6 pupil

The relative invisibility of dyslexia can mean that young people can decide who to disclose the diagnosis to. Sometimes this is an uncomfortable burden of responsibility and pupils often tell us that they would prefer not to have to make that decision.

If you don't tell your friends you've got it, they get upset and ask why you didn't tell them and they say, 'I thought I was your best friend'.

Year 6 pupil

Above all, young people seek social acceptance and want to identify with their peers and not be perceived as different (Harris, 1998). Thus although a diagnosis may confer a legitimacy on their difficulties many recognise that there are consequences to a reliance on a diagnosis, and revealing it to others can lead children to be discriminated against even though their peers may already perceive them to be somehow different.

I have a friend, Jamie. He has dyslexia and my mum thinks I should treat him differently, but I don't. Once we were playing basketball and everything and my mum said I should go easy on him because he has got a disability. I said, 'No, I am winning. I don't want to treat him different'. Everyone thinks you should treat them differently, but I don't. I just treat them the same. And he actually won, so that was really embarrassing for me because he has got a disability.

Year 6 pupil

Weinbren and Gill (1998) write that 'felt stigma may be influenced not only by societal and parental beliefs but also by a feeling of difference and personal insecurity' (p. 68). A number of young people were more positive after receiving coaching or mentoring to help them accept, understand and manage their difficulties.

Well, everybody's different and I'm just different. It is better for me to think like that rather than worrying that I have got a problem.

Year 9 pupil

The gift of dyslexia?

For a number of pupils, the concept of dyslexia is inextricably linked with the idea of a distinct type of reading ability associated with a high IQ although there do not appear to be any studies which substantiate this claim (Frank and Livingston, 2003). Many pupils believe that the typical media dyslexic is almost *always* a very bright individual and for them dyslexia is the 'affliction of geniuses' sometimes referred to as the 'Einstein factor'.

This boy in my class he's dyslexic and the teachers treat him different. But there's another teacher and she says dyslexic people get to be really, really smart. Looking back in history only smart people had dyslexia. Einstein had dyslexia. I think that's the reason people say, 'Oh, dyslexic people are more clever' and stuff like that.

Year 6 pupil

It is not surprising that many pupils tell us that once they have come to terms with their difficulties they develop a perverse pride in using the label.

I take pleasure in telling people I'm dyslexic; it's such a good label – nobody really knows what you mean and I use it with humour about myself because what I'm really saying is I'm clever.

Year 10 pupil

I've got dyslexia now. I thought I just had ADHD [Attention Deficit Hyperactivity Disorder] before but I've just been told I'm psychic. I just feel very happy that I can tell everybody about that I'm psychic.

Year 6 pupil

Further attention needs to be paid to the psychosocial consequences of diagnosis of children with specific learning difficulties.

The social challenge: what we can do about it

Dyslexia can be described as a convenient diagnostic dumping ground allowing practitioners and parents to avoid the messy business of addressing individual learning styles and embracing common responsibility for nurturing and raising confident individuals. Loose diagnostic criteria with no firmly established basis lend themselves to the 'elastic band' effect of ever stretching boundaries. Children can be in danger of becoming objects of descriptions and as a result their creative capacities and diversity can go unnoticed. An over-emphasis on diagnostic labels can push practitioners into self-doubt about their capacity to teach children and therefore opportunities for developing reflexive, creative practices and skills are lost. Children and their parents risk developing tunnel vision about their problems, rendering them unnecessarily disabled and dependent on experts.

An overwhelming emphasis on diagnosis and specialist intervention can lead young people to regard themselves as damaged and can contribute to a negative view of the self. Also the implication that deficits exist in the child may have an unhelpful impact on children's developing self-identity. Locating the problem in the young person may exacerbate their difficulties and give them a sense of being different from others and thus negatively impact upon their confidence and self-worth. There is no doubt that diagnostic labels can be constraining, limiting our view of children's competencies.

Being regarded as disabled may lead in the short term to better relations at home and school, but once a child has a label it becomes difficult to lose it. It is important to be aware that all labels affect children's self-perception and the perception of wider society. Pupils with SpLD may have a range of needs which vary over time and which need to be supported holistically. Children and young people require interventions which will help them to gain a positive view of themselves and also enable them to develop the capacity to be able to locate their difficulties in a broader context.

Dyslexia Friendly Schools

Self-esteem is a crucial issue for all children and young people. A solid sense of self-esteem will enable pupils to be confident about trying new things, get along with others and is at the base of our accomplishments (Lawrence, 1996). It is essential that pupils with SpLD feel that they are succeeding and are valued. Scott (2003) emphasises that distrust of self is an integral part of low self-esteem and that this lack of confidence can emerge from an early incongruence between what children know and feel about what is going on and what others tell them. Such distrust can have the effect of making pupils' difficulties worse and this can set up a vicious circle of inefficiency and unhappiness. Growth in self-esteem is frequently viewed as the most important outcome of the provision which is made available to pupils. Praise and success leading to a positive self-concept can be extrinsic – that is, generated by others such as praise from staff. It can also be intrinsic: when pupils realise that they have been successful and are able to credit themselves with that success, the outcomes can be positive.

The challenge for schools is to create an environment where all pupils feel valued and secure. Recommendations from the British Dyslexia Association's 'Dyslexia Friendly Schools' initiative (BDA, 2005) in which the contribution of the whole-school environment is considered – multi-sensory teaching techniques are standard practice, and where achievement, effort and good behaviour are acknowledged across a range of learning activities – are widely held as being crucial to the well-being of *all* pupils including those with SpLD (Elliott, 2006). One of the fundamental principles of becoming a 'Dyslexia Friendly School' is the expectation that teachers take immediate action when faced with learning needs, rather than referring the pupil for an assessment and waiting for a 'label'. 'This is the policy of *early intervention* being effectively translated into classroom practice' (Elliott, 2006, p. 36). Dyslexia Friendly Schools are effective schools because they identify and select best practice to get the job done. They are empowering schools because they recognise the importance of emotional intelligence.

Peer support group

A peer support group with the development of self-esteem as a central focus can have positive outcomes for pupils with SpLD. The purpose of such a group is not to provide pupils with teaching for improving their literacy skills or as an opportunity to assess the pupils' cognitive functioning. It is important that the group is recognised as an opportunity to develop awareness of the fact that other pupils also experience similar difficulties and as an opportunity to learn how to share and manage feelings of frustration. Difficulties that pupils have previously reported include: 'I can't remember words', 'Everything takes me longer', 'I'm so disorganised', 'My mind is blurry', 'I forget', and, 'I'm having a bad day'. Important steps that can be accomplished in the group are getting over the fear of their difficulties, realising that you can laugh about mistakes, being able to talk about them and working out ways of avoiding the same mistakes in the future. Humour is a helpful tool and within a structured group it is possible to take advantage of its healing effects. It is important to enable younger pupils to benefit from the experiences of older pupils and thus encourage pupils to believe that they too can become successful learners.

A solution-focused approach

A group can also encourage the adoption of a more reflective and evaluative approach to the choice and use of strategies for improving their literacy and organisational skills and for managing their learning differences. A structured group can enable pupils to reframe their attitude towards situations and learn how to focus creatively on solutions rather than emphasising the *rigidity* of the problem. The courage and 'can do' attitude that can be created in a group can encourage pupils to take risks in how they negotiate the world.

Something to say

One of the most important things a group can achieve is to help the pupils explore ways of talking to others about their difficulties, and encourage them to be able to explain succinctly what they need from others. Encouraging pupils to develop simple phrases to use and uncomplicated explanation of their difficulties will assist them as they encounter new people and situations. It will also enable pupils to feel more at ease with their individual learning styles. Explanations might include: 'You may have to speak slowly or write things down for me because I have difficulty processing and writing information'.

Celebrating success

Giving up a familiar stance takes confidence, especially where there are others with a stake in the pupil maintaining a 'helpless' role (particularly parents). A carefully structured group can help pupils to visualise success and celebrate each other's successes. It is important that the pupils sign up to a fixed number of sessions over a term. In our experience a series of five sessions, each lasting for forty-five minutes, spread over one term is most effective.

Building relationships

Pupils who are encouraged to see their SpLD as a learning difference, and to understand that it conveys a range of strengths and weaknesses, will begin to value the advantages and experiences it can bring. In turn these pupils will begin to respect themselves just as they are. Being accepted for who we are is an important component in good self-esteem. Scott (2003) emphasises that a route to helping to renegotiate a sense of self is through relationships with others that are both truthful and straight. He suggests that it is better to say 'OK, you have some problems. Let's look at how you can deal with them' (p. 90). The most powerful phrase is 'I believe that you can do these things differently'.

What's really going on?

A good relationship with significant others – whether a teacher, teaching assistant or learning mentor – can do a great deal to challenge low self-esteem and the negative and destructive self-talk that goes with it. It is therefore important that adults take the time to build relationships with pupils and, instead of accepting challenging behaviour at face value, take the time to understand what is really going on. Pupils may present as being over adapted to the needs of others, at great pains to fit in and do exactly what they think others want them to do. This sort of passive behaviour can mask low self-esteem and a lack of strong personal identity. Alternatively there is the aggressive stance of pupils who convey an attitude of 'I don't care what you think' and are frequently labelled as having social, emotional and behavioural difficulties. Scott (2003) suggests that staff may be taken in by these defensive behaviours and not be aware of the feelings of failure and vulnerability beneath.

Praise

Young people have identified that the teachers they thought helped them best gave them lots of praise and positive reinforcement for their efforts. Some teachers, however, might argue that praise alone is not sufficient and that it is a disservice not to draw attention to areas of weakness and how they can be improved. A helpful approach is to give as much positive feedback as possible while simultaneously addressing a manageable number of basic errors.

> *My teacher always tells me what I have done well. She says I write really good stories. She will point out one or two things I need to work on and give me a worksheet to practise. Then she says that I will get a star if I remember next time I write a story. She puts a label on my desk to help me remember what I need to remember.*
>
> *Year 5 pupil*

It is important that specific difficulties are addressed within the context of highly positive feedback and that pupils are given explicit 'small step' strategies for dealing with difficulties so that they can feel they have some control rather than feeling overwhelmed by their mistakes. Young people need to know what they can do well and what they can realistically do about their mistakes. As pupils get older it may be possible to negotiate with them how they would prefer to be given feedback.

Teachers need to review practices which publicly highlight a child's difficulties, in particular expecting them to read aloud or reading out all the pupils' results in a spelling test. It is important that verbal contributions are valued as highly as written contributions both in terms of classroom practice and in terms of assessing a pupil's strengths.

Nothing succeeds like success

The most powerful contribution to improving self-esteem and confidence is success. Improved performance in literacy skills are of course important, but any success – whether in sport, design, information technology, music – can lead to confidence, the willingness to take risks and put pupils in touch with their own strengths and sense of self-worth.

The learning environment: what young people tell us

Specific learning difficulties can be described as a distinctive pattern of learning difficulties that are particularly, though not by any means exclusively, associated with the acquisition of reading and spelling skills. Pupils may also have accompanying weaknesses in short-term memory, sequencing and the speed at which they process information. These are the key skills that everyone needs if they are to learn effectively in a busy classroom and it is not surprising therefore that pupils tell us that underachievement is probably the most frustrating aspect of their difficulties and that this frustration affects not only themselves but also those who teach them. The emphasis in schools on learning and achieving and the importance of proving ability through written examinations has been criticised by a recent report by the Social Market Foundation (2006) which confirms that if the curriculum is to meet the needs of the whole person as a physical, moral, social and intellectual being, it cannot be a curriculum that focuses on a narrow range of skills and knowledge or one that requires pupils to spend most of their time reading and writing.

Reading

Reading is an important life skill and there is a strong link between fluent reading and academic success. It is also for many people a source of pleasure and a means of finding out about topics of interest. Yet reading is often a problem area for pupils and is almost always effortful and the cause of embarrassment and anxiety. Many pupils tell us how hard it is for them to learn to read.

> I can't see a whole word at one time when I look at it. It's like I see only one letter at a time in my name. First the 'd' then 'o' then 'g' but I don't know what the whole word means because I can't see it all at once. So I try to connect each of the letters in my mind one by one. But I can't always do that because by the time I connect the last letter, I've already forgotten what the beginning ones were.
>
> *Year 4 pupil*

Even when pupils have learnt to read, however, poor perceptual skills mean that they find it difficult to see letters in the correct order and keep their place when reading. They may continue to experience difficulties with the mechanics of accessing print and therefore their reading may appear to be hesitant or laboured.

> Sometimes when I read I get dizzy and nauseous. My mum tells me that it's like that for her when she tries to read in a car which is going over a bumpy road. The letters and words get lost when I go to read them and they bounce about and get twisted and turned and chopped and reversed and they are all blurry.
>
> *Year 8 pupil*

Other pupils tell us that once learnt they cannot remember a word for very long and so later when they see that word again they have completely forgotten what it was.

> I see words jumbled up in a different kind of way so it is very hard for me to remember them. I learn a word and then next time I see it I don't recognise what it is. It is like I have never seen that word before in my life. The lesson I find the hardest is English because I've got to do all this reading and writing and it just really tires me out.
>
> *Year 7 pupil*

Other pupils may have age appropriate reading skills but their reading may continue to be laboriously difficult and characterised by loss of place in the text, omitted lines or repetition of the same line which will inevitably affect their understanding of the text.

> When I go to read, my eyes keep losing their place. So I skip words and sentences and I keep rereading the same words and sentences over and over again. Then I see words that aren't there. And I miss words that are there.
>
> *Year 8 pupil*

Although pupils may develop strategies to manage their reading difficulties these can be time consuming and make the pupil appear to have the reading ability of a much younger child.

> It helps to use a finger or ruler when I read. That way my eyes know where to come back to when they start jumping around, losing their place. I also seem to be able to read better when I hold a book close to my face. And when the letters are big and black and easy to see.
>
> *Year 9 pupil*

Spelling

A common misunderstanding is that if a pupil can read a word, then they ought to be able to spell it; however, this is not the case.

> I learn the words for a spelling test but then I go and forget the words just after a test. I think spellings just can't stick in my mind. Sometimes I can get the spellings right in my head for a test but then when the test is finished the spellings are gone.
>
> *Year 5 pupil*

Pupils' work may be characterised by the same word spelt differently in the same piece of work, confusion between upper- and lower-case letters and concepts of letter name and sounds. The confusion of similar letters ('b' and 'd', 'p' and 'q', 'w' and 'm') result in bizarre spellings and, as emphasised in the previous section, children and young people with spelling difficulties can often be labelled as lazy or careless.

I can't even remember what simple words look like when I have to spell them. And I can't remember the sounds of letters and words in my mind. My mind just goes blank. I have to picture and sound out each letter at a time in my mind and then I have to put them all together. But when I'm thinking about one letter I forget all the others.

Year 7 pupil

I read, write and spell things upside-down and backwards too. Once a teacher said to me, 'You make the same stupid, dumb writing mistakes over and over. Can't you remember a 'b' and a 'd', and words like 'was' and 'saw'? You are the slowest girl I've ever taught and other staff have told me the same thing.'

Year 8 pupil

I have to ask for spellings all the time, if I want to get them right and the teacher writes them on the board, which makes the rest of the class think how stupid I am.

Year 6 pupil

Writing

For many pupils there is a marked disparity between their spoken and written language. These pupils usually appear as able as their peers at many things until, for example, they need to write something down.

I have 4 peaol in my famley,
I have 2cuts ay 1dog
I live ina huse

(Transcript of writing by a Year 7 pupil who was asked to write for five minutes on the topic 'My Family'.)

The work that they produce is often badly set out, with spelling mistakes, crossings out and handwriting that looks heavy and laborious. Pupils tell us that they write their letters back to front or the wrong way around and write 'd' for 'b' and 'p' for 'q', 't' for 'f' and 'u' for 'n' because they find it difficult to see the differences in these letters and almost impossible to remember which way round they should go when they are writing. Apart from not being able to remember spellings pupils tell us that they find handwriting and the ability to control a pen or pencil very difficult.

I can't write straight. The letters get big and small. The words go up and down. The spacing is big and small. Uneven. Sometimes I even begin writing from right to left. At times I can't even remember how to write the shape of the letters and then I just skip letters. Even when I'm writing my name I start writing [and] I leave letters out. It's like I can't learn to write the letters in sequence. First I have to write one letter, then another, then another but [the] problem is my mind goes faster than my hand. So I think I've written things I haven't; other times it's the opposite – my hand just sort of gets stuck writing the same letter over and over again.

Year 7 pupil

Sometimes my hands shake. I think its because I hold the pencil so tight. But if I don't hold it tight, I'm scared I won't have any control over where it's going and what I'm writing.

Year 5 pupil

Copying

Pupils tell us that they find it exceptionally difficult to copy written work from the board and this, coupled with problems with organisation and concentration, can mean that they struggle to keep up with the pace of lessons and miss out on processing and recording important information such as homework, which is a task which is usually left until the end of the lesson.

I have problems with the blackboard and it's after four periods of work. The teachers haven't wiped it properly and it's really hard to focus, the colours blend in with each other. The whiteboard is OK but when you get the light reflecting off it you can't see the word. It's much better to copy something next to me, rather than off the board.

Year 9 pupil

People talk and make too much noise and I can't hear the teacher and the teacher's writing on the board. It doesn't help when he keeps rubbing it out and when I tell him he says you should work faster and teachers don't let me finish copying; they rub it out so quickly.

Year 8 pupil

When the bell goes, the teacher writes on the board. I'm writing then another class is coming in at the same time and I have to rush it down. When I get home I don't understand what I've written because I've rushed it so I don't understand the homework.

Year 8 pupil

Organisation and planning

Pupils also tell us that they find it very hard to organise their thoughts when they are asked to write a story or an essay. Pupils tell us that they find it difficult to get started or their minds fill with a jumble of ideas that it is difficult to get down into any order. They lose the thread of the argument, go off at tangents and the more they keep writing the more muddled the piece gets. Writing becomes a cycle of diminishing returns and this, combined with their spelling and handwriting problems, can mean that writing is an activity which they dread.

> *The lesson I find the hardest is English because you have loads of writing. I get upset when I can't write stories or poems as good as other people. I have difficulties with Geography and History too because in those lessons I am also expected to write a lot of stuff and I never know what to write about first. My teacher always tells me write a beginning and a middle and an end but I can't work those things out. My brain just won't do it because I can't think ahead. I also can't spell lots of words and I can't write fast.*
>
> *Year 8 pupil*

> *When I'm writing there are problems for me with putting down things in the right order and I can't put down ideas on paper properly. It's not laziness. I have a problem with my memory, holding on to information as I'm working something out. I can't do more than one thing at a time: first I have to work out what I want to say, then I have to hold on to it and then I have to spell the words.*
>
> *Year 9 pupil*

Examinations

Examinations and tests are an important part of school life; however, they are events which are dreaded by many pupils because they demand skills that some find difficult such as recalling information, the need to organise one's thoughts and get one's ideas down on paper coherently, quickly, legibly.

> *The worst things about school are reading and tests. I especially hate tests because I know the answer but I can't read the questions. And so I can't answer anything right. Then I get very frustrated with myself and feel so stupid. I could do much better if I was asked questions and allowed to answer them out loud.*
>
> *Year 8 pupil*

Pupils tell us that their results often do not reflect their abilities and the whole process can throw a dark shadow over their life at school. A number of pupils are entitled to 'exam arrangements' such as an amanuensis and the use of a word processor, which they value highly; however, the provision of additional time in examinations for some pupils is experienced as a burden.

> *I don't want extra time to sit in that room not knowing what to do. What's the point of extra time if I can't remember what to do and I haven't got any information to write down? When everybody else has gone I just sit there feeling guilty because I don't know how to fill the time.*
>
> *Year 10 pupil*

The learning environment: what we can do about it

Pupils with specific learning difficulties can reach both academic and personal goals provided that their needs are recognised and they are appropriately taught. Reid (2005) emphasises that despite evidence to the contrary there is 'no specific approach that is universally recognised to deal with dyslexia' (p. 7). Responsibility for teaching pupils with SpLD therefore lies not with a 'specialist' or 'expert' but firmly with class or subject teachers who have the knowledge and experience of adapting and differentiating materials and are able to adapt their teaching to meet the needs of individual learners. The needs of these pupils can be met as much through careful planning of curriculum and teaching objectives as through the use of specialised materials. Knowledge of teaching and learning strategies rather than access to resources are key (Elliott, 2006). It is important that teachers have knowledge and a real understanding of the types of difficulties pupils are likely to experience and can then match this with a knowledge of the profile of individual pupils (background, difficulties, strengths) and the strategies that have already been put in place for these pupils. Placing the focus on learning in the mainstream classroom offers the possibility of improving the quality and quantity of discrete intervention and can lead to opportunities for more higher quality intervention. In dyslexia friendly schools, the focus has changed from establishing what is wrong with pupils in order to make them 'better' to identifying what is right in the classroom in order to enhance the effectiveness of learning.

Assessment

Reid (2005) emphasises that knowledge of each individual learner is essential as the profile of strengths and difficulties presented by pupils can differ widely. Assessment practices, however, are usually associated with normalisation, classification and categorisation of a pupil's learning difficulties. The power balance is firmly tipped towards the adult who has a pre-set agenda. An emphasis on the negative implies that something is wrong with the pupil and leads to a focus on identifying weaknesses rather than celebrating strengths. When experiencing negative emotions and feelings of incompetence individuals usually fall back on what they know is safe at the cost of blocking out expansiveness and new learning.

Learning Difference

The concept of 'learning difference' (BDA, 2005) on the other hand conveys a range of strengths and weaknesses. If each pupil is to be truly respected as an individual learner with a unique learning style, then it is essential that the purpose of assessment practices are redefined as being to notice, recognise and respond to competent learners and communicators. It is important that children and young people have a larger part to play in defining and communicating their individual learning styles and identifying their signature strengths (Seligman,

2002). Recognition of strengths and competencies can function to broaden and build cognitive and social resources. How does this happen? Positive emotion generates exploration which in turn allows mastery. Mastery itself produces more positive emotion, creating an upward spiral of good feeling, more mastery and more good feeling (Seligman, 2002).

Reading for meaning

'Literacy implies more than reading' (Reid, 2005, p. 43). The purpose of reading is not as Elliott (2006) emphasises to decode which is a low level skill but to ensure that the reader comprehends the message that is contained in the text, which may not be explicitly stated by the writer but arrived at by inference on the part of the reader. The implication for practitioners is that they need to do more than train pupils to become skilled decoders. In order to become independent readers, pupils need to be able to work out what the text means, know how to use the text in the immediate context and also understand how the text has been constructed to produce specific effects on the reader. First and foremost, then, it is important that pupils with SpLD are not, as Reid (2005) emphasises, 'rooted into tedious instruction and practice in decoding which would mean that the higher order skills implied in critical literacy are neglected' (p. 43). Unfortunately an emphasis on the difficulties involved in teaching pupils to decode has resulted in the widespread belief that reading is acquired by strictly logical means for strictly logical purposes and almost entirely by formal, sequential teaching. Teaching 'harder', however, does not address persistent learning difficulties. Teaching differently does. Nurturing pupils' motivation to learn and their enjoyment of reading is as important as teaching the underpinning skills.

The Matthew Effect

Baylis (2005) suggests that children who start off reading well will get better and better compared to their peers, because they will read ever more broadly and quickly. The more words they read, the easier and more enjoyable it all becomes. On the other hand, it's very hard for poor readers to catch up, because for them the spiral goes down. The Matthew Effect (taken from a passage in the gospel of St Matthew, 25.29) is based on the belief that an initial success in something tends to lead to even greater success and if we are unsuccessful, we are likely to become even less so. Baylis suggests that success or failure will 'grow like Topsy' (p. 87) whichever gets the upper hand first. Due to the Matthew Effect, the gap between those who read well and those who read poorly may grow bigger rather than smaller without appropriate intervention.

'Catch Up'

'Catch Up', a structured literacy intervention programme for pupils who find reading and writing difficult, was developed at Oxford Brookes University in

1998 and is now in use in over 4,000 primary schools over the UK. It is a proven and effective tool for helping struggling readers during short, twice weekly sessions. The programme integrates reading and writing and develops word recognition and phonic knowledge, spelling and also comprehension and fluency. Emphasising the reading process as a continual interaction between the reader's language experience and understanding of the world ensures that pupils enjoy reading and develop the literacy skills that can be effectively generalised into other situations.

Phonemic awareness

There is currently agreement that in an alphabetic language such as English, phonics teaching is essential. Without at least some grasp of phonics, children are unlikely to learn to read (Palmer, 2006). For children to be able to benefit from phonics teaching they have to be able to distinguish the individual speech sounds (phonemes) of their native language which is an ability usually acquired long before children start school. Songs, rhymes, laughter and conversation with a loved one are far more effective ways of preparing a child to read than a phonological training schedule. If phonemic awareness isn't acquired naturally at this very early stage, it can be very difficult for children to develop it later. The sections of the brain which are involved in processing speech sounds have now been identified and it has been established that for some children genetic factors make it difficult to discriminate certain phonemes. Other children may have poor phonemic awareness because they don't get enough exposure to language in the early years; hence the importance of talking, singing and rhyming with very small children. Once they reach school age if children are unable to discriminate speech sounds, they are less well equipped to read than their peers. Palmer (2006) writes that researchers are now looking at ways to identify which sounds pupils cannot distinguish (as it will vary from child to child) and train them to recognise these sounds. However, learning to process speech sounds is only one tiny facet of reading and relying on intensive phonological training schedules without attending to the wider picture could end up doing more harm than good.

> **Joe**
>
> Joe, a Year 3 pupil with significant reading difficulties, was happy to read out text alone even in assembly when he had the opportunity to prepare and practise it at home with adult support. The class teacher made sure that Joe's reading was limited to a comfortable amount. Joe's teaching assistant pre-read texts with Joe and used this opportunity to familiarise him with specific vocabulary. Another supportive strategy, which gave Joe confidence when he was reading in class, was to allow him to read together with other pupils. Choral speaking can be a successful way of encouraging reluctant readers. Joe also had access to a personal CD, which he used during silent reading sessions to listen to taped stories, which he followed in a book. He particularly enjoyed the audio assisted Rainbow Reading Scheme and the non-fiction books

which comprise 50 per cent of the scheme. This self-pacing individual programme improved Joe's attitude to reading, boosted his confidence and fostered his independence.

The class teacher also trained a more competent peer to be Joe's study buddy. Activities the pupils shared included paired reading and checking each other's spellings. As Joe had excellent football skills and was a valued member of the school team his study buddy benefited socially from Joe's status in the playground.

Metacognition

Metacognition means thinking about thinking (Peer and Reid, 2001). It has an important role in learning and can help to develop thinking skills and enhance the pupil's awareness of the learning process. Reid (2005) suggests that pupils with SpLD often make poor use of metacognitive strategies. This can mean that their learning is not efficient and that they may take a long time to learn new information. This is because they are not able to effectively access previous information or work out how they learnt. Teachers therefore have a key role to play in assessing metacognitive awareness and encouraging its development (Peer and Reid, 2001). Pupils need to be encouraged to reflect on what they are doing and why they are doing it. Encouraging pupils to ask themselves the following questions during tasks can provide a structured framework for learning.

- ▸ Purpose: Why am I doing this?
- ▸ Outcome: What do I need to produce at the end?
- ▸ Strategy: How should I do this?
- ▸ Monitoring: Am I being successful and is what I am doing successful?
- ▸ Development: How can this be improved?
- ▸ Transfer: How can I use what I am doing in other situations?

Examinations

Examinations are often very difficult for pupils with SpLD. Metacognitive factors have particular relevance to examinations because success involves being aware of the task and the processes involved in completing the task. Pupils frequently do not understand what examiners are looking for in response to the questions that are set in exams; however, a metacognitive approach – analysing exemplar answers and knowing, for example, that a three-mark question demands three clear sentences written on separate lines rather than a rambling paragraph – can be very helpful. Teaching pupils to be able to manage time during examinations is also vital.

Learning styles

All pupils learn best when their strengths and difficulties are recognised by their teachers, when they are taught to their preferred learning styles and when they have some control over their learning. Learning is a dynamic process; different parts of the brain interact with other parts and each relies on and interacts with the other. The various parts of the brain that deal with vision, hearing, memory, understanding and co-ordination may be all used simultaneously to complete a task. Frequently it is this synchronising of learning skills that is challenging for pupils. The notion of multi-sensory approaches involving the use of visual, auditory, kinaesthetic and tactile strategies are believed to be essential for all learners.

A multi-sensory approach

A multi-sensory approach means that the stronger channel or modality can be used to support the weaker, while at the same time the weaker channel is being trained and developed. In order to accentuate pupils' strengths, teaching programmes should be multi-sensory and incorporate visual, auditory, kinaesthetic and tactile approaches. Material that is presented in a multi-sensory way has a better chance of being remembered. Tasks therefore need to be carefully structured, simplified and focused towards the pupil's preferred learning style. Pupils with SpLD are usually stronger visually or kinaesthetically (Reid, 2005). Initial learning will therefore be more meaningful if it is presented visually or kinaesthetically. Well-presented visual material is vital. Worksheets need to be clearly printed, well spaced, with clearly labelled diagrams and illustrations and at an appropriate reading level. Enlarged print may be beneficial in reducing visual stress and pastel coloured paper will reduce glare.

Multi-sensory techniques can be used during reading and spelling to integrate the learning of the sound of the letter, its shape on the written page and the feel of writing it in cursive script, so that a secure sound–symbol relationship can be established. Pupils usually find spelling more difficult than reading and therefore by linking the two, spelling is encouraged by reading.

Simultaneous oral spelling

Simultaneous oral spelling is a popular and widely recognised multi-sensory technique. The pupil says the word, then spells it aloud, then writes it while saying the word aloud and finally checks it. The sensory input is that pupils hear and feel themselves saying the word, they hear the sequence of letters, they hear them again while feeling their hands write the shapes. Pupils then see the word appear on the page and can compare it with the original, for a final visual input.

Helen

Helen, a Year 7 pupil, could read at an age appropriate level but struggled to spell words. Lists of key words were always on the board at the beginning of lessons and lists of the same key words were printed on cream paper, laminated, and available on the desks. The teacher did not comment on or correct misspellings except those which had been taught or provided. Written work was marked on its content so that pupils would not become inhibited and unwilling to produce creative work. Parents were informed of this marking policy.

As Helen had a good phonological ability (i.e. she could segment words into syllables and phonemes and spell alphabetically), it was decided to provide her with an 'ACE-spelling dictionary'.

Helen needed direct instruction in how to use the spelling dictionary. This was taught as a group activity and the pupils were given practice in developing their ACE dictionary skills.

The group were taught that the most important thing to understand is to listen to the way you say a word. First of all, the pupils identified the first phoneme in the target spelling word. Then the pupils worked out the first vowel sound. The helpful pictures in the dictionary prompted the pupils (e.g. cat for 'a', eagle for 'ee', owl for 'ow', shark for 'ar'). The pupils used these two references in the index to locate the page number. When they found the correct page number, they counted the number of syllables in the word. On the page, they looked at the columns for one, two and three syllables indicated by asterisks (* = one syllable, **** = four syllables and so on). Under the correct number of syllables, the words are listed alphabetically in columns. Even though Helen found spelling difficult, she was soon able to find any word she needed quickly and efficiently.

The pupils were also taught to use the dictionary for proof-reading their work, rather than looking up words as they wrote. This strategy ensured that the pupils concentrated on content, rather than on the secretarial aspects of writing. When their draft written work was completed they identified likely spelling mistakes and used the spelling dictionary to correct their work.

Helen's parents have bought an ACE dictionary for Helen to use at home. Helen's family are poor spellers and Helen has shown them how to use the ACE-spelling dictionary and thus the whole family have benefited from this resource.

ACE dictionaries are available from the LDA website which is listed at the end of this chapter.

Organising study

Being organised is a basic and vital skill which depends on four basic rules. These are:

▸ Plan and prepare

▸ Work in stages

▸ Take things slowly and steadily

▸ Take regular breaks.

Organisation can pose particular problems for pupils with SpLD and therefore instead of asking open-ended questions such as, 'What was the story about?', providing a structure or organisational framework in which to retell the story can enable the pupil to organise the information into categories such as characters, plot, location, ending or conclusion. Encouraging pupils to organise information into a number of component parts is a fundamental aspect of the Talking Partners approach (Kotler *et al.*, 2001). Pupils are provided with cue cards or prompt sheets for activities such as news telling, story telling or picture descriptions to help them organise their verbal contributions during group activities. An organisational framework makes it easier for pupils to retell information orally and therefore retain new information.

Over-learning

Pupils with SpLD require an increased amount of over-learning or reinforcement of what they have been taught. This means, in effect, that a range of teaching approaches are used to ensure that the same words or skills are being taught in different situations. If a new word is, for example, learnt in one lesson, it is important that this same word is also used in other contexts and the connections are emphasised to the learner. Over-learning can apply to spelling rules and many spelling patterns lend themselves to over-learning through the use of the pattern in different words.

Mnemonics

Mnemonics can be auditory, visual or both auditory and visual. Auditory mnemonics may take the form of rhyming and alliteration while visual mnemonics can be used by relating the material to be remembered to a familiar scene, such as the classroom.

Clarifying instructions

Pupils with SpLD may very easily misunderstand or forget information that is given to them. It is essential for teachers to ensure that pupils have understood instructions. This is helped by keeping instructions short and, if at all possible, giving pupils a demonstration of what the task entails. .

> *Explain, then ask if I understood. If not, explain with pictures etc. Write things down clearly and teach the basic information without rambling on about other things. But if I do understand, then don't overdo it so that it becomes boring.*
>
> *Year 11 pupil*

Provide copies of notes, information, homework

A key factor in enabling pupils to be organised is to ensure that they have the correct information. Expecting pupils with SpLD to rely on notes or information that they have taken down from the board or from dictation is likely to cause difficulties because of their reduced working memories and/or their motor control difficulties; their writing may be slow, hesitant and illegible. Pupils tell us that one of the most helpful things teachers can do, especially at high school, is to provide them with hand-outs which contain the information that they need for the lesson. If the hand-outs can be distributed to the whole class, there is less likelihood that pupils with SpLD will feel singled out. A well-presented hand-out will enable pupils to focus on the content of the lesson rather than worrying about taking notes and keeping up with the teacher. It is important for teachers to be aware that expecting pupils to summarise what they are saying is usually not realistic.

Copying from the board

Copying from the board is often very difficult for pupils and should be kept to a minimum or avoided altogether. Incorrect versions of what is written on the board may make a pupil appear careless, but in fact short-term memory or spatial difficulties mean that pupils easily lose their place or 'jump' lines. If a small amount of copying is unavoidable, it is important to ensure that pupils are seated in a position where they are facing the board, as having to turn around can be disorientating and exacerbate short-term memory difficulties. The minimum amount of information should be written on each line. Numbering each line and writing lines in different colours can also ease the task of copying. The writing should be clear and should stay up as long as possible. One high school, in their pursuit of Dyslexia Friendly School status, banned all copying from the board for one week. Staff reported afterwards that they regarded this as a worthwhile exercise as many teachers were forced to rethink lesson delivery and present information in a more accessible manner. The pupils enjoyed policing the week and ensured that no teacher broke the 'no copying' rule.

Homework

It is important to ensure that pupils understand what homework they have to do by asking them to explain it in their own words to the teacher or to a teaching assistant. Writing the homework on the board at the beginning of a lesson or providing a photocopy of homework for all pupils can minimise or avoid the difficulties some pupils experience. It is important to find out how long it takes pupils to complete homework and then, if necessary, adjust the amount of homework accordingly so that it can be completed in a reasonable time according to the pupil's age and stage of development. Pupils with SpLD may take many more hours to complete homework than their peers.

Information technology

It is important that pupils have access to age appropriate electronic tools such as a spell checkers. For many pupils access to a simple word processor can be invaluable.

With my Alphasmart I don't have a problem and my hands fly over the keys (in class they say you can see the steam rising!) – typing comes naturally to me now, like writing does for other people, and with the spell checker, I can spell the words. The one thing it doesn't help me with is confusing words that sound alike: I often put 'witch' instead of 'which', 'no' instead of 'know' and 'past' instead of 'passed'.

I'm not trying to say it's a miracle cure, because it is not. You have to work constantly, but the word processor will give you skills that will help you in later life. I think my word processor is the best thing that has ever happened to me and I would recommend it to anyone.

Year 8 pupil

Access to a word processor will be of limited benefit if a child does not have access to an age appropriate touch-typing program and regular practice time. The children need to learn the layout of the keyboard, accurate typing and then progress to improving their typing speed. Age appropriate typing tutor programs can be used in a classroom with headphones. Older children may benefit from access to Voice Activated programs.

Conclusion

The Dyslexia Friendly Schools initiative (BDA, 2005) has done much to ensure that specific learning difficulties are not seen as a within-child deficit but as a responsibility of the school and one that needs to be shared positively by all members of staff. It is hoped that this chapter will provide practitioners with an awareness of the implications of SpLD for both curriculum development and the classroom environment.

Useful websites

www.LDAlearning.com

www.gamzuk.com

www.bdadyslexia.org.uk

www.interdys.org

www.dyslexiaaction.org.uk

www.dyslexic.org.uk

www.catchup.org.uk

Chapter 5

Including Pupils with Hearing Impairment

Dr Ruth M. MacConville
Janet Palmer

Introduction

Hearing impairment is a clinical term used to describe all types and degrees of hearing loss. Throughout this chapter the terms 'deaf' and 'hearing impaired' are used interchangeably and refer to the whole range of hearing loss. This reflects common practice in the field of the education of the deaf and also the personal preference of the authors. Hearing impairment can be defined as any loss of sound sensitivity produced by abnormality anywhere in the auditory system. There are two main types of deafness of which conductive deafness is the most common. Sounds cannot pass through the outer and middle ear to the cochlea and auditory nerve in the inner ear. This is often caused by fluid in the middle ear (glue ear). It is estimated that between 15% and 20% of children between two and seven years of age are affected (Peer, 2005). Glue ear is a temporary condition and hearing levels often fluctuate from day to day. It usually clears up naturally but can develop into a long-term condition requiring surgery. The second type, sensori-neural (nerve) deafness, is a permanent condition associated with a malfunctioning of the inner ear. Sensori-neural deafness may be passed down in families or caused by infectious diseases such as rubella, mumps or meningitis. There are different degrees of deafness; they are classified as mild, moderate, severe or profound. Few children are totally deaf; most can hear some sounds at certain pitches and volume and all deaf children experience sounds differently. Although a more significant hearing loss is likely to result in more severe difficulties this is not always the case; there are many deaf pupils who make excellent progress in all areas of the curriculum and serve as a reminder of the importance of maintaining high expectations.

According to the National Deaf Children's Society (2006) there are approximately 34,000 deaf children in England. Hopwood (2003) estimates that over 85 per cent of deaf pupils now attend mainstream schools; however, the figure is much lower for those with a profound loss who are likely to attend a school for the deaf. The majority of deaf pupils attending mainstream schools communicate through spoken English, using their residual (remaining) hearing through hearing aids and speech reading (Powers, 1999).

Hearing loss can be described as an invisible acoustic filter that distorts, smears or eliminates incoming sounds, especially sounds from a distance – even a very short distance. Pupils with a disability which is not apparent to the casual observer face a complex situation. On the one hand, they do not automatically attract attention, as might be the case if their disability was obvious; on the other hand, they may not gain the support and understanding they need. Where pupils are affected by an invisible disability such as deafness they may feel reluctant to draw attention to their condition, even though they may be unable, without certain adaptations, to meet some of the basic social expectations of others. Although a hearing loss itself is invisible and therefore easily ignored or underestimated its effects are often wide-reaching and pervasive. They are highlighted in the two personal accounts which follow, both of which were written by deaf pupils attending mainstream schools. The first account is written in the form of a letter by a Year 8 pupil called Rosa. The second is by Paul, a Year 11 pupil.

Personal accounts

Rosa, aged 13

This account is an exact transcript of a letter written to a peripatetic (visiting) teacher of the deaf. The difficulties that deaf children have with language are inevitably reflected in their writing. In the following account these difficulties are conveyed by the use of shorter and frequently incomplete sentences, omission of articles and prepositions, errors in verb tenses, and by a restricted vocabulary.

Dear Miss (sorry I don't know your name),

There something I always wanted to tell you but somehow I never got it out of my mouth, so I am writing to you so there no stopping. Well, I am a loner. And I hate. Once I sat with my sister friend and they were so much fun and the time went by so quickly. That's what I want. A friendship of my own. I know now why I never had non-deaf friend because in primary there was a group of deaf people and we been close friend since nursery.

What I am saying is that I want to go to a deaf school. Very badly. Even my best friend who is in a deaf school seem to have a lot of friends. Ever since in the middle of Y7 I wanted to go to a deaf school. I know I have to sleep there but I love that idea but I don't my parent would agree to it. They don't know how much pain I am in. I had try so many time trying to make friend even in different groups but it didn't work. Most of the time I'm very upset but I am good at hiding them.

If I am be able to go to a deaf school I will be the most happiest girl in the world, it would be like a dream come true. And if I don't I know soon I going to go out of control. Sometime I feel like I want to shout, scream and cry and laugh all at once, in the middle of the lesson and go crazy. I get so jealous of the people who have close friendship. So if you could help me please do so.

PS Don't mention it on Friday lunchtime cause usually I burst into tears while I am telling the story.

PS Can we talk about this at break cause I'm cooking food so we won't be able to go in the small room at 11 o'clock. What to you say. Oh no I have to do cooking at break (to set thing up). When you have time them we can talk.

Paul

My name is Paul and I go to a mainstream school. I'm in Year 11 and I am going to tell you what it's like being deaf for me. The real problem is not so much that I can't hear; it's about not knowing what's going on.

In my brother Tom's bedroom every day the snooze alarm wakes him and then while he's still half asleep he hears the news and the weather check. He registers to take a coat to school because it's going to rain. Flick! A light switch is being switched on in the hall and he hears the shower running and a door being bolted. 'Cool', thinks Tom, 'there's going to be another ten minutes in bed.' Tom hears the kettle switch off and the toaster 'pop'. 'Great, breakfast is under way'.

I'm usually woken up by a vibrating alarm clock which goes under my pillow and bounces my head to make me wake up. It's broken at the moment and so I'm woken by mum shouting, 'Get up' and pulling the duvet off me. I can't even hear an alarm clock. Even when I put on my hearing aids I don't hear what's going on. For me there is only Mum shouting, 'Don't forget your PE kit', 'Feed the cat', 'Help your brother take out the rubbish'.

By the time I get to school, there has already been a problem on the bus because the driver couldn't understand what I was saying. When I get to school I look for Ali my friend. I don't want to join in with any of the groups because it's embarrassing if I don't get what they are saying. All I can see are mouths moving. I say 'Hi' and walk on but I just smile if they say anything else to me.

I don't hear the bell ring but I get it's time to go in when I see the others walking in. At lunchtime it's noisy in the canteen when I sit down to eat my packed lunch. I think the others are talking about *Little Britain* but I can't really follow what they're saying. I'm glad when it's home time. For me being deaf is like being a visitor in a foreign country. I can get some of what is going on but there's lots I miss. I can't join in groups and I miss jokes. It's hard to relax in school because I work on making myself look like I belong and what is being said to me all the time.

The social challenge: what young people tell us

The development of our spoken language depends upon hearing the speech of others. Deafness can therefore adversely affect language development, especially if the child has been deaf since birth, and the chances of misunderstandings occurring during everyday interactions are far greater than for other pupils. It is common, therefore, for deaf pupils to experience feelings of isolation and care must be taken to nurture their emotional and social development. As these personal accounts highlight, a great deal of what we know about the world is acquired through 'incidental' learning – learning which happens spontaneously. We overhear conversations and pick up information and misinformation without even thinking about it. Deaf pupils, even those with minimal hearing losses cannot detect intelligible speech from a distance. This reduction in 'earshot' has significant and negative consequences for both social and emotional development and classroom learning. Flexer (1999) emphasises that 90 per cent of what young children know about spoken language and the world they learn incidentally. The deaf child has to be taught directly much of the vocabulary and knowledge that other children learn incidentally. Deaf children frequently do not know the latest slang expressions or understand jokes, riddles or verbal analogies and this lack of knowledge acts as a barrier to their effective communication, particularly with their peers in a social context. We learn from talking to deaf pupils that their everyday communication is often fraught with misunderstanding and that they experience the constant anxiety that not being able to hear will be 'read' as not having understood.

What would you feel like if you had to keep asking people to say something again and again? Even the shortest thing they say I sometimes don't get. They get tired of me not hearing what they're saying and usually end up telling me to 'Forget it'. That makes me feel like they want to forget me.

Year 10 pupil

It can be difficult because they are all talking together, telling a joke and I can't hear ... and so I say 'yeah' and laugh, or I laugh real loud so everybody thinks I've got the joke and then everyone looks at me as though I'm a freak.

Year 9 pupil

Audible but not intelligible

One of the most frustrating things pupils report about being deaf is the fact that their deafness does not mean a complete absence of sound; rather it means that they can hear some frequencies better than others and that many sounds are distorted. For speech to be intelligible, the person must be able to discriminate the word–sound distinctions of individual phonemes or speech sounds. Ross (1991) emphasises that the major problem with having a hearing loss is that you can't hear so good not that you can't hear at all. Consequently speech might be audible but not consistently intelligible to a child with even a mild hearing loss, causing the child to hear, for example, words such as 'walking', 'walker' and 'walks' all as 'ah'. This can give the impression that the hearing loss is selective and that deaf pupils can hear when they want to, when it suits them.

They didn't sort out I was deaf until I was three years old; they thought that because I could hear music on the TV and the door bell my hearing was OK. When I wasn't starting to talk my mum got worried and took me to the doctors. Now it's the same in school: because I can hear the door bang or have learnt to expect when my name is going to be called on the register teachers think I can hear. The point is I can only hear sometimes – like when it's quiet and the teacher has put stuff on the board so I can read at the same time, then I know what she's on about. I can hear when my best friend and I have a chat on our own but if it's noisy like in the playground or in the dining hall I usually haven't got a clue what people are on about, but because I can hear the bell for registration the teacher tells me I can hear when I want to and when it's convenient for me. That is so annoying.

Year 7 pupil

In reality, for many pupils their hearing loss means that they can hear if the listening conditions are favourable; if there are very low levels of background noise and if the context is clear. It is also helpful if pupils can predict what the conversation is going to be about.

Lip reading

Pupils who are deaf, even those who are moderately deaf, tell us they are dependent on watching faces and 'reading' body language to supplement what they can hear:

I always make sure I am sitting where I can see my friend's face so I can look at her lips and try and work out what she is saying. I don't always get it right but if I can't see her face, I'm lost and I can't work out what she's saying at all.

Year 5 pupil

Lip reading involves watching a person's mouth and face in order to 'read' what words are being said. It depends on a knowledge of the grammar and vocabulary of the language because you cannot lip read a word that you do not know. Pupils tell us that lip reading is very 'tricky' and requires their full concentration. This is because in order for words to be recognised by their lip patterns, sounds must be formed at the front of the mouth. As most consonants are articulated at the back of the mouth even an experienced lip reader will only be able to accurately lip read about one-third of what is being said. Most deaf individuals cannot lip read that well (Gregory and Hartley, 1994).

Lip reading is a little bit like doing a fill-in-the-blanks test. Some words are 'visible' and have the same mouth movement; they look the same on the lips but sound different. I make so many mistakes because I have to guess what my friends are saying. One time I thought they were talking about Care Bears but they were on about going to the fair.

Year 11 pupil

Hearing aids

Pupils with significant levels of hearing loss will usually be fitted with post-aural (behind the ear) hearing aids. It is usually advantageous for children to be fitted with two hearing aids. Amplification to both ears means that there is a stronger likelihood that the hearing aid wearer will be able to locate sounds and also be able to distinguish the speaker's voice against background noise. The benefits of wearing hearing aids vary considerably from person to person according to a range of factors.

> *The first things I would save in a fire would not be sentimental things, they would be two small, pink hearing aids. Without them I would, as an audiologist put it, be a 'psychological jelly fish' – isolated and incapable of communication with the rest of the world.*
>
> *Year 12 pupil*

Other pupils tell us that hearing aids do not help them and that they just cannot wait to stop wearing them.

> *I've told my dad when I get to be 17 I am going to stop wearing my aids. I can't hear much with them on … all I hear is crackles. When I get to 17 I don't care what my dad says, I'm throwing them out. If I could, I would have done it before. Hearing aids just give me vertigo.*
>
> *Year 9 pupil*

We learn that it is sometimes tempting for pupils to reject their hearing aids because, despite tremendous technological advances, hearing aids cannot fully restore hearing to normal.

> *Even my new digital aids can't cope with sounds over a certain decibel level. They stop filtering sound and instead develop a high-pitched whine. Leaving them in is like listening to a succession of jet planes landing right next to me.*
>
> *Year 12 pupil*

Hearing aids are most useful when the speaker is within one metre of the hearing aid wearer and there is a quiet listening environment.

Looking different

Although hearing aids can improve hearing they also mean that pupils may be singled out as being different and are likely to be questioned about being deaf by their peers. Many pupils tell us that they experience their hearing aids as 'making them different'. Allan (1999) describes hearing aids as being 'co-ercive markers of a disability' (p. 89). Pupils describe the conflict they feel when wearing their hearing aids in school and tell us that even though they sometimes help them to hear better they dislike the negative comments that they attract from their peers. Pupils tell us that they grow their hair long to hide their aids and practise putting them on and removing them inconspicuously to avoid attention. Pupils tell us that a frequent taunt is that they should not be wearing hearing aids because they are for 'old' people and that they are sharing an ailment more usually associated with older people. Only about 2% of young adults are deaf or hard of hearing but in people over 60 that rises to 55%.

> It's much better [wearing my hearing aid]. I can hear some of the words on the TV and what is said to me – it's much sharper and clear ... but it's just in school everybody will stare and think I'm different and they [other pupils] tell me they [hearing aids] are only for old people.
>
> *Year 11 pupil*

Transition

Pupils tell us that were often far more comfortable wearing their hearing aids in the familiar environment of the primary school but that they rejected them during the transition to secondary school.

> Oh yes, I liked my new [secondary] school – it looked really cool, but I didn't hear much of what he [head teacher] said because I didn't wear my hearing aids. I didn't want them to know I am deaf. They might not want me if they know I can't hear ... I don't know why I need to wear them every day anyway ... I am going to practise listening without them.
>
> *Year 6 pupil*

Pupils tell us that they were unprepared for the attention that wearing hearing aids attracted from a new peer group.

> The kids all come up to me and shout and try to touch my hearing aids. I push them away but they say, 'Why have you got them in your ears?'
>
> *Year 7 pupil*

> When I first came to this [secondary] school I felt scared, worried and different. It took time for me to get along at this school, meeting new teachers and new friends. In this school some people are interested to know what it is like being deaf, while other people just stare at you wondering what's wrong. They make me feel angry and insecure; they are being nosey.
>
> *Year 7 pupil*

Deaf pride

Some pupils, however, tell us that they wear their hearing aids with pride and prefer to be 'upfront' about their deafness. They tell us that they prefer to wear brightly coloured, conspicuous hearing aids so that people quickly see that they are deaf and speak more clearly to them.

> *Then Nicky joined our school. Nicky has two bright yellow hearing aids and she has short hair. She doesn't grow her hair long like me to cover up her aids. Nicky has a bigger hearing loss than me and she tells people she is deaf. Nicky talks really loudly and I think people are sometimes a little bit afraid of her – she has strong opinions.*
>
> *Year 8 pupil*

Only for learning

Other pupils report that they wear their hearing aids 'only for learning' because they feel under pressure from staff to do so.

> *When Miss [form tutor] comes to see me in class I put them [hearing aids] on. I said I wore them most of the time and it was OK. But one day she turned up in French and I was really worried because I didn't have them on and I was sitting at the back of the class. At the end of the lesson – which I thought went quite well – she asked me some questions and I realised that I had missed out on lots of stuff. We talked about me wearing my hearing aids and I promised to wear them for English and for Maths.*
>
> *Year 7 pupil*

Fitting in

Pupils, especially in secondary schools, often refuse to wear their hearing aids because they believe that the anonymity that this gives them will help them to 'fit in' socially.

> *I'm happy because my hearing aids got broken and had to be sent away to be fixed. My friends forget that I am deaf when I don't wear my aids. I pretend I understand them when they talk to me and nod and smile and then they continue talking and think that I am understanding them. There's no point keep saying 'pardon' or asking them what they're talking about because I wouldn't understand them anyway.*
>
> *Year 7 pupil*

Although without hearing aids deaf pupils may look indistinguishable from their peers communication becomes even more problematic. Pupils tell us that they frequently lose the thread of a conversation and learn the art of carrying on chatting without really understanding what the conversation is about. Nods and smiles enable the dialogue to continue and when asked a direct question deaf pupils tell us that they usually reply with a neutral answer such as 'Really?' or 'I'm not sure'. This evasive behaviour, being unassertive and lacking persuasiveness in conversations encourages further forgetfulness of their deafness among their peers. Corker (1994) describes this behaviour as 'behaving like a chameleon which changes colour to hide from predators' (p. 56).

Group conversations

Deaf pupils repeatedly express their frustration at feeling 'left out' of group conversations and describe the reluctance of their peers to help them understand what is going on.

> *My aids work well, but they can't cover all situations. I still walk out of a room just as somebody starts speaking to me. I still fail to respond to a question and miss important conversational links. It's one thing to fall out with people but another to simply offend half the people you meet, usually without even noticing you are doing it.*
>
> *Year 12 pupil*

For the deaf pupil group conversations are much less predictable and therefore much more difficult to engage in than two-way conversations. This is because there is not the basic pattern of a listener for each speaker and the identity of the next speaker is not known. There are also far more interruptions and more than one speaker competing for a turn in the conversation. A potential speaker has to monitor the conversation closely in order to secure an opportunity to speak. The strategies that speakers use in order to secure a turn in the conversation, such as overlap (talking over the current speaker) and interruption, are very difficult for the deaf pupil who also has to follow the conversation as it moves from person to person and constantly work out who is speaking. Chunks of conversation may be missed, therefore, while the deaf person 'searches' for the speaker. Pupils tell us that it is unusual for their peers to take on a 'traffic director' role for deaf pupils during fast-paced peer exchanges. We learn from listening to pupils that their deafness can undermine their desire to become part of a group. Without others to talk to and with limited opportunities to rehearse all the behaviours necessary for social development, deaf pupils are at risk of becoming increasingly confused and isolated.

> *I can't always follow things; it's not even that I'm really deaf – I'm just a bit deaf but even so I can't really follow what they [peers] are saying and then they think I'm just thick, then I get upset. I can't think of anything to say except talk about football.*
>
> *Year 8 pupil*

Social knowledge

A large part of understanding one's own and other people's emotions is learnt through conversation. Children gain an understanding of other people by talking about what they believe other people are thinking. It is not surprising, then, that pupils often report feelings of isolation and that there are often significant gaps in their social knowledge which can result in social immaturity. One of the biggest challenges hearing impaired pupils tell us they face in school is their social adaptation – the ability to get along easily with others and make friends. We learn from listening to pupils that they are significantly more likely to be neglected by their peers and less likely to have a friend in school. Nunes *et al.* (2001) emphasise that inclusion must be assessed in terms of its social consequence for pupils. If deaf pupils feel isolated in school, their education is likely to suffer. Studies suggest deaf adults who attended special schools report far more positive recollections of school than those who were educated in mainstream schools (Gregory and Knight, 1998). Pupils who have experienced different types of provision often report a strong preference for special schools or units.

> *I've never had a non-deaf friend because in primary [school] there was a unit and a group of deaf people and we had all been close friends since nursery.*
>
> *Year 9 pupil*

> *All my friends are deaf too so we talk and sometimes use BSL [British Sign Language].*
>
> *Year 8 pupil*

This expressed preference for a deaf friend matches the findings of Gregory and Knight's (1998) study in which deaf pupils emphasised that 'there shouldn't be one deaf pupil on their own in a class of hearing pupils but four or five [deaf pupils] in each class', (p. 64). In this same study pupils expressed their 'tension and frustration' (p. 64) about being placed on their own in a mainstream class. Similarly, Lloyd *et al.* (2001) found that both deaf and hearing pupils prefer to interact with peers of the same hearing status.

The social challenge: what we can do about it

There is a growing body of evidence that promoting social and emotional development should be a core component of ensuring that deaf children achieve their academic potential. As we have already emphasised in the first chapter of this book good social and emotional functioning is strongly associated with academic achievement. When addressing the social and emotional needs of deaf children we have found it helpful to draw on the framework of the cycle of development and the associated developmental affirmations (Clarke and Dawson, 1998) because these children are at greater risk of developing mental health needs than their hearing peers (Hindley *et al.*, 1994).

Too much information

The vast majority of deaf children are born into hearing families with little or no previous experience of deafness (Hindley and Reed, 1999). Technological advances in the detection of deafness at the earliest stages following birth mean that parents often receive the news that their child is deaf almost immediately after the child is born. Many parents have told us that for them this was 'too much information' which interfered with the early bonding process.

Fletcher (1987), the parent of a deaf child, writes about 'information overload' at the time of diagnosis and the need to establish a balance for parents between wanting information and their ability to retain it. Parents tell us that they go home from hospital with a small baby, understanding little about deafness, feeling alone and not knowing how they feel or what to do to help. 'At diagnosis there is often confusion, stress, and impaired bonding' (NDCS, 1999). For other parents there may be a wait from the time they begin to suspect something is wrong until deafness is confirmed. The process of diagnosis means that parents may not able to give their child the unconditional, positive affirmation 'I'm glad you are you'. Parents tell us that they have found it difficult to talk naturally to their deaf baby because they are consumed with worry that their the baby may not be hearing them.

The emotional impact on a family on discovering that they have a deaf child has been well documented. Family reactions are typically negative, emotional and very strong although it is important to appreciate that family reactions are individual and variable (Corker, 1994). It is estimated that 81 per cent of hearing parents never learn how to communicate effectively with their deaf child and therefore these children are more likely to be impulsive, have limited problem-solving skills and have greater difficulty in identifying and naming their own and other people's emotional states (Greenberg and Kushe, 1993). Deaf children who have deaf parents, on the other hand, are likely to have had a natural and uninterrupted communication within the family from birth.

The cycle of development

The ambivalent behaviours of deaf pupils who are reluctant to wear their hearing aids or who are at pains to conceal their deafness suggest to us that these children may not have achieved the key developmental tasks associated with the earliest 'being' stage of the cycle of development. Pupils who fail to signal their needs or get help in times of distress are also letting us know that they have not completed important early developmental tasks. Allan (1999) describes pupils who seek to hide their deafness and have not had their deaf identity valued by the school as being 'characterized by tension and fear of discovery' (p. 92).

Trusting relationships

What does this mean for the staff in schools? It is important for staff to learn about the likely effects of a hearing loss before meeting a hearing-impaired pupil for the first time in order to avoid the potential pitfall of creating an ambiguous and confused relationship. Learning about a pupil's disability does not mean becoming an expert; it means knowing enough to fulfil one's responsibilities to the pupil. Deaf pupils are likely to have already been assessed and it makes sense to check whether there is information already available in the school.

Letting the pupil know you know

Welcoming the pupil and letting the pupil know that you know about their deafness is an essential first step and will hopefully enable pupils to acknowledge their deafness to themselves and then to others. As Allan (1999) emphasises, 'pupils need to be helped to cope with the real situations in which they find themselves ... rather than being viewed through the normalizing gaze of a professional in a certain role' (p. 116).

One-to-one conversations

In order to successfully include pupils with hearing impairment it is important for staff to understand that all degrees of hearing loss can have a significant effect upon interpersonal communication. When we engage in one-to-one conversations with pupils with moderate hearing losses most present very little apparent difficulty and appear to have no problem in comprehending the speaker and in making appropriate responses. In such a situation, the child appears to have a choice of vocabulary and language structures and is able to select those with which they are familiar and which seem appropriate to the situation. This is true of all of us as we only tap in to a small percentage of our language knowledge in any conversational exchange. If, however, one were to carry on an extended conversation with these pupils, particularly about topics removed from their experiences, and listen carefully to what the pupils were saying, a less optimistic picture may emerge. It would soon become obvious that these pupils have much less flexible options in how to express themselves. The skilled listener would soon detect the presence of a number of pervasive language problems, one of the most important and underestimated of which is a paucity of vocabulary. A great deal of everyday conversation is made up of idiomatic and metaphoric expressions, slang and colloquialisms which the deaf child may not be familiar with.

Taking the time to engage in one-to-one conversations with a deaf pupil is important and will help to ensure that a rapport is established. Such exchanges are much easier for the deaf child because the topic is usually chosen by the two people involved and as the deaf individual has only one other person on whom to focus, the potential for losing track of what is being said and missing information during the conversation is reduced. In a one-to-one conversation it is also much easier to 'repair' the conversation or sort out a misunderstanding as only one person has to backtrack and clarify what was said.

Peer support groups

Peer support groups are an effective way of providing structured, time-bound support for deaf pupils and provide a psychologically 'safe place' for pupils to explore issues associated with their disability.

Conditions for success

Facilitators

Staff need to be given time to develop their skills as facilitators and have opportunities to evaluate and reflect upon their experience. Facilitators need to have some understanding of the rules of group work and basic counselling skills. Coppock and Dwivedi (1993) highlight the need for staff awareness of the differences between the role of the teacher and the role of the facilitator. Ainscow (1999) has argued that it should not be necessary for schools to reach outside for expertise in order to meet the needs of pupils with disabilities; however, staff in schools have told us that they value the opportunity to work with a member of the specialist team when running groups, especially for the first time, and that without this initial partnership approach they would not have the knowledge or skills to be able to disambiguate the pupils in matters relating to understanding their deafness. Nor would they have fully understood the significance of pupils' expressions of confusion and ambivalence about their deafness.

Strategic approach

Support groups need to be recognised as part of an overall planned approach to meeting pupils' social and emotional needs (Gross and White, 2003). In practical terms this means the provision of an appropriate room and the regular, planned release of staff.

Pupil Involvement

Greenhalg (1996) emphasises the importance of pupil involvement and choice. Pupils need to be able to choose whether they wish to take part. Chalk and Smith (1995) emphasise the importance of the 'socialisation process that is embarked upon by group members once the climate for caring, trust and growth' is established in the group. Pupils tell us that it is extremely important to them that they have contact with other deaf pupils and that although they are usually surrounded by hearing peers, most would prefer to spend more time in relationships with other deaf pupils which they describe as being deeper and more satisfying. Studies confirm that hearing-impaired students have more positive perceptions about their relationships with their hearing-impaired peers than with hearing ones (Stinson et al., 1996). Setting up a peer support group specifically for deaf pupils can prevent or reduce the pupils' sense of isolation, mobilise mutual support and provide opportunities for the group to acknowledge each other's needs and experiences.

It's good to know there are other people with hearing aids. I thought I was the only one in my school, it feels comfortable.

Year 9 pupil

Peer support groups can also enhance social skills, self-esteem and enable deaf pupils to manage feelings and improve a sense of interdependence as well as autonomy. Thomas and O'Kane (1998) emphasise the importance of using a participatory approach to running a group and adopting a conversational style, which allows the pupils ownership of the content and direction of the group. A support group offers pupils the opportunity to take an active part in group discussions. For most deaf pupils this is an unusual occurrence. Agreed ground rules such as one person speaking at a time and no interruptions can support communication and smooth running of the group.

The facilitator can by gaze or unobtrusive gesture quickly direct deaf pupils' attention to the next speaker so that chunks of the conversation are not lost. For the deaf pupil a support group can help to dispel feelings of social isolation. Hargreaves (1994) emphasises that a sense of self arises from the social experience of interacting with others. It is usual for pupils once the group is established to begin to express anger and powerful feelings of extreme frustration that they are deaf:

It's not fair I can't hear so good. My brother and sister can and I think why me? At times I feel angry and I could stab my pencil into people ... they make me so angry.

Year 7 pupil

In terms of the cycle of development such disclosures indicate that that pupils have reached the 'thinking' stage of their social and emotional development. Developmental tasks at this stage include asserting an identity that is separate from others, acquiring information about self, expressing anger and frustration. It is essential that staff do not discount these powerful expressions of feelings but instead provide pupils with positive affirmations such as, 'All of your feelings are OK with me' or 'It's OK for you to be angry'. Helpful adult behaviours which will accelerate the work of the group include expecting pupils to express feelings and to connect feelings and thinking, to continue to be supportive as the pupils explore ideas and feelings, and to provide information about the pupils' environment and to give answers to their questions.

For many pupils a deaf support group is the first opportunity they have had to openly reflect upon their deafness and consider what it means for their identity. A group can provide opportunities for discussing experiences and concerns shared specifically by hearing pupils. Pupils with hearing loss do not necessarily understand the impact of their deafness and need to have an understanding of their own identity and be able to accept their deafness before they can fully problem solve issues that occur because of their disability.

Terminology

An issue that deaf pupils frequently seek to explore is how to describe their deafness – what words to use. For a number of pupils, especially those with more moderate hearing losses who do not want to be described as deaf, the term 'hearing impaired' is preferable. When this term was originally introduced it was considered to be a more positive term than 'deafness' because it emphasises the fact that the pupil has some remaining hearing.

Big D and little d

The term 'hearing impaired' is not generally used by deaf people themselves because of its negative connotations. A number of pupils will therefore prefer to use the term 'Deaf' to describe themselves. The use of a capital or 'big D' as it is usually described denotes that they do not consider themselves as disabled because they lack one of their senses; rather they view British Sign Language (BSL) as its replacement. The Deaf community view themselves as a linguistic minority who are proud of their unique heritage and willing to fight for it. The majority of hearing-impaired pupils who attend mainstream schools, however, are likely to describe themselves as deaf with a 'little d', denoting the medical model of deafness as a disability.

It is important for staff running support groups to understand these contrasting views of deafness and to be aware that although the term 'hearing impaired' is usually accepted as standard terminology, for some pupils it may convey undesirable nuances (Bienvenu, 1985). It is essential that pupils have the opportunity to explore the terminology that is associated with deafness and are able to make their own informed and individual decisions about which term to use to describe their disability.

> *Me and Nadia and Miss meet every week to talk. Sometimes Sally joins us. Sally doesn't wear hearing aids as she is only a little bit deaf. Sometimes Lisa joins us too … her mum and dad are both Deaf with a capital D and she calls herself a CODA [child of Deaf adult]. Lisa says they choose not to wear hearing aids because they are adults and use BSL at home. Lisa has been signing since she was born and says the worst thing about being a CODA is that sometimes people talk to her and ignore her parents. She says that makes her feel mixed up inside, but her parents don't mind. Lisa says she would shout at people. I would be like Lisa's parents and not say anything. We talk about lots of different things in our group and we moan about things. I really enjoy the group.*
>
> *Year 8 pupil*

Although teachers of the deaf have retained their name since its inception and work with pupils with the full range of hearing loss, it is important that staff be aware that pupils may react strongly against some terms and in dialogue with pupils adopt the terminology which is preferred by the pupils themselves.

The following case study illustrates the benefits of running a group for pupils with a range of hearing losses in a primary school. This case study emphasises that a support group can benefit not only pupils with severe deafness but also those pupils with moderate losses or unilateral (one-sided) deafness.

Taking Control: a support group for deaf children

'Taking Control' took place in a mainstream primary school over the course of one term. The group met regularly on Friday lunchtimes and was facilitated by a peripatetic (visiting) teacher of the deaf and teaching assistant. Four pupils attended the group. Ali, a Year 4 pupil, had a unilateral hearing loss and had recently undergone a tymplastogram (repair of the ear drum). Although he appeared to be working well in the classroom his teacher was concerned about Ali's low levels of self-esteem and his anger which 'spilled out' during Circle Time. Beth, a Year 3 pupil, also had a unilateral hearing loss and complained regularly to her teachers about her frustration with her classmates who did not understand that she could not hear them when they shouted to her across the playground. Carl, a Year 2 pupil, suffered from 'glue ear' which meant that his levels of hearing fluctuated from day to day. Carl told his teacher that he often felt as though he was 'listening with his fingers in his ears'. Danny, a Year 3 Pupil, wore two hearing aids and had a sensori-neural hearing loss.

Discussion during the first meeting of the group focused on the medical aspects of the pupils' deafness, what had happened to them at diagnosis, Ali's operations, and Danny's experience of being fitted with hearing aids. From discussion during subsequent meetings it became clear that the four pupils had the following factors in common. Each believed they were the only pupil in the school with a hearing loss; all reported that they often felt angry, sad, frustrated and lonely in school; none of these pupils understood their hearing loss or had talked about it to anybody before. During the sessions pupils shared their frustrations about being deaf, of people not helping or understanding them and also the positive aspects of being deaf.

> You can get away with not doing your homework because you can say you didn't hear them.

By the end of the term, the pupils reported that they were beginning to 'Take Control' of their deafness and that they no longer felt isolated and had drawn considerable strength from being part of the group. The pupils also reported that they were able to apply the strategies they had learnt in the group.

> When I don't understand in the classroom I ask the teacher to explain it to me again.

Friendship

Peer support groups enable pupils to share their experiences and opinions with peers whom they may not have otherwise come into contact with and therefore increase their social repertoire. Thompson et al. (2001) write that 'groups are the highways of childhood' (p. 11) and that 'big secondary schools are the motorways' (p. 12). Although pupils often tell us that they do not feel part of the 'in' group they also report that one of the advantages of attending a mainstream school is that they value being aware of what is happening in the 'fast lane' (p. 13). Thompson et al. (2001) observe that friendship resembles the side streets and back roads. Friends can go at their own pace, stop when they want to and get away from 'speeding traffic' i.e. the 'in crowd'. Deaf pupils emphasise the importance of having a friend in school and preferably a friend who is also deaf, somebody who they can talk to and who understands them. Without at least one strong affective bond – a friend – pupils will experience loneliness and isolation (Hartup, 1996). This confirms the findings of Sullivan's (1953) classic study of friendship, i.e. that 'chums' provide an essential source of social experience and support for each other. Proximity is one of the vital antecedents of friendship and therefore the more we can enable pupils to interact with each other and share experiences, the more they are likely to build a positive social climate and develop friendships (MacConville and Rae, 2006).

The learning environment: what pupils tell us

Deaf children, even those with mild/moderate hearing losses, frequently experience difficulties with listening in the classroom. They usually do not have the linguistic or auditory experience to enable them to grasp the content of what is being said and therefore cannot compensate for the distorted version they hear of what the teacher is saying.

> I can't follow what teacher's saying, especially when she walks about [the classroom] and I can't see her face.
>
> *Year 5 pupil*

> I don't like it when my teacher stands in front of the window and talks to us. The light is so bright I can't see his face. Watching his face helps me work out what he is saying.
>
> *Year 7 pupil*

Divided attention

Hearing-impaired pupils tell us that they are dependent on watching faces and reading body language for information. They rely on important cues from facial expressions, lip patterns and natural gestures to supplement the incomplete or unclear version of what is being said. As Bathurst (2005) emphasises, the diminution of one sense traditionally amplifies another. 'I listen with all my strength. I listen not just with what remains of my hearing, but with my eyes and my instincts. I see sounds I hear with the whole of me' (p. 20).

Deaf pupils report that they frequently have to divide their attention between listening to the teacher and the task in hand.

> When Miss is reading a book out loud to the class she asks us to read the story in our own books at the same time. I can read the story in my book or I can listen to the teacher. I can't do both the things at the same time. If I look down at my book, I can't hear her [teacher]. If I look at her and listen, I can't read my own book.
>
> *Year 7 pupil*

> When we [pupils] are in the computer room we are all sitting around the room looking at the computers. I can't look at the computer and hear what the teacher is saying because I can't see her face to help me hear her. I just work it out myself or ask someone next to me how to do it.
>
> *Year 6 pupil*

Listening difficulties are exacerbated in noisy listening conditions.

> I can't hear in class because the [classroom] door is always left open and there are always people walking up and down [the corridor]. All I can hear are footsteps and the chairs in my classroom. When they [other pupils] drag their chairs that is all I can hear, same as when they bang [cupboard doors] or drop books that is all I can hear.
>
> *Year 6 pupil*

Pupils can also be affected by subtle sounds which can be particularly disturbing to hearing aid users.

> I was always listening to a funny noise in class. I didn't know what it was but it was really annoying and then I worked out it was the long electric light over my desk which was sort of humming all day long and my hearing aid just made that sound louder and louder. I got a headache from it and then I asked if I could move to another seat away from that noise. She [teacher] said I could.
>
> *Year 5 pupil*

Support exchange

One of the responses to pupils' listening difficulties is the provision of a teaching assistant (TA). Pupils tell us that sometimes it can be confusing to have a TA explain what the teacher is saying.

> The teacher's talking and all the time Miss [TA] is sitting near me telling me what she [teacher] is saying. It is hard for me to look at both [of them]. I want to know what the teacher is saying but I'm supposed to look at Miss [TA]. I can't follow two of them together.
>
> *Year 7 pupil*

Hopwood (2003) refers to the process of more than one adult inputting to the deaf pupil in the mainstream as 'support exchange' (p. 86) and writes that this may cause the deaf pupil some difficulty as they may be unsure whom they are supposed to be listening to. This is exacerbated by the fact that it is very difficult for deaf pupils to tune in to and pick out different parts of different conversations simultaneously.

The negative attitudes towards support that were expressed to us by many secondary aged pupils reflect the attitude that many pupils have in not wanting to be singled out from the class as being different or put 'in the limelight' and made to feel unacceptably different from their hearing peers. A particular difficulty that pupils reported was the fact that they receive signed versions of what the teacher is saying even though they described themselves as not being 'signers'.

> It's easier for Miss [TA] to sign to me what the teachers are saying because then she [TA] is not disturbing the class, but it is hard for me 'cos I don't really sign. I talk.
>
> *Year 9 pupil*

Pupils often tell us that they sometimes pretend to understand what the teacher is saying rather than admit that they are having difficulties. Pupils tell us that they prefer not to ask for help.

> It's embarrassing and then sometimes Miss [TA] starts to sign at me 'cos she knows I don't know what Miss [teacher] is on about; it's easier for her [TA] to sign 'cos it's embarrassing for her talking at the same time as the teacher.
>
> *Year 9 pupil*

On entering school deaf pupils may have much smaller vocabularies, more restricted world knowledge and experiences and more limited inferencing skills than their hearing peers (Lewis, 1998). This gap tends to widen as pupils get older as deaf pupils can miss out on so much incidental learning which is critical for development. Hence by the time deaf pupils have made the transition to high school they are often linguistically ill equipped to deal with the secondary curriculum.

Although 'amplification technology' (hearing aids, radio aids, sound field systems, cochlear implants) can improve hearing it cannot restore a deaf child's hearing to normal. The expectation that wearing a hearing aid makes their hearing normal can be very frustrating for pupils.

> They [teachers] think that a hearing aid gives you back your hearing. I had textiles with a teacher who saw my hearing aids and then started shouting at me. She made me cry 'cos I didn't understand what she was saying and she thought I could hear her.
>
> *Year 9 pupil*

Pupils tell us that staff must know that they are deaf because they are wearing a hearing aid or using a radio aid; however, the effects of the hearing loss are still easily ignored or underestimated by staff.

> My form tutor said to me, 'I know you have got a hearing problem but will you please just listen to me properly'. He just didn't understand that even though I was wearing a hearing aid and a radio aid I still couldn't hear him properly.
>
> Year 8 pupil

Other pupils tell us that teachers don't understand what a hearing loss is all about because they seem to think that a raised voice will enable the deaf pupil to take a full part in the lesson.

> Some of them [teachers] don't understand [my deafness] – they just go to your face and talk really very loud; but there are some who are really good and they give out notes which help me understand what they are talking about.
>
> Year 9 pupil

Radio aids

Many pupils with severe and profound deafness are likely to be equipped with Frequency Modulated (FM) radio systems which are usually referred to as 'radio aids'. Radio aids were developed in order to overcome some of the limitations of personal hearing aids, particularly in terms of distance between the speaker and the hearing aid wearer and reduction of background noise.

> Sometimes in assembly I turn it off, especially in the boring bits. But it's good that I can choose [what I want to hear]. Before I just didn't hear at all and I thought I was missing something; now I know I'm not.
>
> Year 8 pupil

Radio aids consist of a small receiver worn by the pupil and a transmitter with a microphone worn by the teacher. Pupils have to remember to collect the transmitter and microphone from the teacher at the end of every lesson and then take them to the next lesson. Despite major technological advances in the design of radio aids their efficacy depends upon the teacher wearing the microphone correctly near to the mouth and the pupil remembering to collect the microphone at the end of each lesson and giving it to the next teacher.

> I get late to every lesson because I have to wait until the end for Miss to give me the microphone and then I have to run to where I'm going next and so I'm late every time.
>
> Year 10 pupil

Cochlear implants

An increasing number of pupils are being fitted with cochlear implants. This is a device which provides direct electronic stimulation to the cochlear in the inner ear, through electrodes. It is estimated that a normally hearing child has approximately 12,000 cochlear hair cells transmitting vibrations to the auditory nerve and on to the brain. A profoundly deaf child, on the other hand, might only have 1,000 hair cells which means that they may derive very little benefit from wearing a hearing aid. A cochlear implant bypasses the inner ear mechanism and sends messages directly to the brain via an electrical circuit. Using the device involves surgery to implant a receiver and electrodes in the individual's head and additionally the person has to wear a microphone, transmitter and speech processor. The microphone which is at ear level picks up speech and other sounds which are then converted into electrical signals which are conveyed to the implanted receiver.

Pupils tell us that cochlear implants 'help them to hear more' but do not fully restore their hearing and that after the implant operation they need to relearn how to listen and make sense of sounds that they are hearing for the first time.

> I had my cochlear implant when I was in Year 3. I don't remember a lot about listening before the operation. I used to have two hearing aids that I wore every day. You don't hear straightaway after the operation – they [hospital staff] wait a while before they switch it on. I just knew I had all these things put inside my head. When they switched on my implant I do remember everything sounding different. [There were] a lot of bangs and sounds that made me jump and it was very confusing. I thought that after the operation I would be able to hear like my mum and my brother but it isn't like that. I had to work really hard at learning to listen and sometimes I got really fed up. I used to say it was easier when I had my hearing aid because I didn't have to listen all the time. Sometimes it was difficult knowing if it was someone talking or if it was just a noise. My mum said she was just so pleased when I noticed the telephone ringing – I didn't know it was the telephone; to me it was just a noise I didn't know. I did lots and lots of listening work. Some of it was fun like picking out sounds. Some of it was really hard and I really had to think. Up to then I hadn't really thought about all the sounds as I watched people a lot. At night I take my implant off and then it all goes quiet. Sometimes I take it off when I am tired and want quiet. Noise can be so tiring.

> *Year 5 pupil*

Older pupils are often reluctant to have a cochlear implant as Bathurst (2005) comments: 'I don't like the idea of becoming profoundly deaf, but at the moment I can work with what I've got. Besides I reckon I want radical surgery as much as I want a hole in the head' (p. 20).

The learning environment: what we can do about it

Deafness, first and foremost, can have a significant impact on a child's speech and language development . Even a mild or moderate hearing loss can mean that information cannot always be gained reliably and effectively through listening. To the child with a hearing loss conversational speech is usually not clear and listening is adversely affected by environmental influences such as distance from the speaker and level of background noise. It follows, therefore, that one of the most startling difficulties that deaf children often face is a lack of an awareness of language and consequently gaps in their knowledge. A deaf child may have a limited vocabulary and not be aware of colloquialisms, as we only usually know words which we have learnt through use. Deaf pupils are, however, usually very skilled at disguising gaps in their knowledge and are often reluctant to admit that they do not know an answer to a question or have not understood. Ask a deaf pupil 'Do you understand?' and they will inevitably answer 'yes'. They will, however, usually not be able to answer a more searching question on the topic in hand. Pupils tell us that part of their reluctance to admit that they do not know the answer to a question is their lack of confidence that even if the question or information is repeated they are not confident that they will understand.

It is important to emphasise that the negative effects of a hearing loss on speech and language development are not restricted to pupils with a significant hearing loss. A moderate, temporary loss of hearing has been recognised as a significant factor in pupils who are underachieving in school and even when the intermittent hearing loss has cleared up, the secondary effects of the hearing loss will remain. The link between glue ear (known to affect between 15% and 20% of children between two and seven years of age) and subsequent reading difficulties has been well established. Pupils with restricted literacy skills frequently have a history of early hearing loss (Peer, 2005).

Despite the fact that deaf pupils represent a diverse range of individuals, the difficulties they tell us that they experience in school fall fairly neatly into three main categories. These include difficulties following teacher talk; feelings of isolation because of inability to join in or even follow group discussion; and enduring distressing levels of extraneous noise.

Difficulties following teacher talk

Deaf pupils, even those with moderate hearing losses, cannot detect intelligible speech from a distance. A child who is learning to interpret speech needs to hear *all* the sounds clearly in order to develop effective speech and language skills. An absence of information such as linguistic boundaries, plurals, tenses, intonation and stress patterns will inhibit a child's language development. Strong links have been shown between a moderate hearing loss and immature speech sounds, limited vocabulary and sentence structure, poor comprehension of spoken language, and difficulties in discriminating and sequencing (Peer, 2005). An adult, on the other hand, does not have to hear all the speech sounds in order to put together the concept of what is being said. Speech can be badly distorted or interrupted and still be intelligible to an adult because all the contextual strategies of processing speech are usually fully established.

Classroom management

In the classroom, the general principles for teaching a class that includes a deaf pupil are based on common sense and include ensuring that a pupil has a preferential seating position towards the front of the class and providing plenty of visual clues and written information to support listening.

Classroom acoustics

Attention to the acoustics of the classroom can significantly enhance the listening environment. The challenges of maintaining attention and perceiving speech are exacerbated in classrooms where there are high ceilings, bare floors and walls. In such environments sounds will tend to reverberate, i.e. bounce off hard surfaces and become muddled, which will significantly compound pupils' listening difficulties. Sound-absorbent materials such as acoustic tiles, carpets, soft furnishings, curtains and rubber caps on chair and table legs will cut down on reverberation and unwanted noise.

Preferential seating

It is important that from an early age pupils with hearing loss are encouraged to sit in a position near to the teacher and where they cannot only see the teacher's face but also the faces of the other pupils in order to be able to lip read them. A seat to one side of the class towards the front usually gives the best vantage. It is important to encourage the pupil from an early age to be involved in choosing their own preferential seating position. Pupils will be able to listen more attentively to the teacher and to each other in quiet areas away from sources of constant sound such as a library area.

A multi-sensory approach

Using a multi-sensory teaching approach means enabling a pupil to learn through more than one of the senses. Ensuring that information and instructions are duplicated in another format that does not depend on hearing (e.g. on an interactive whiteboard or worksheet) and that lesson aims and key words are clearly written on the board from the beginning of lessons, will support *all* pupils.

> *I didn't want a helper [TA] with me all day so in my school the teachers do lesson plans and lesson notes for me instead. These are given out to the whole class, not just to me, so I don't feel different. Everybody likes getting these notes – they help us to understand and remember what the teacher said. I'm lucky; they should do that for everybody who's deaf.*

> *Year 10 pupil*

For younger pupils who are developing phonological awareness, a multi-sensory approach will enhance the development of early literacy. Involving the use of sight touch and movement will give the pupil's brain tactile and kinetic memories which will re-inforce memory and enhance learning (Peer, 2005).

Group discussion

Deaf children in mainstream classes frequently face communication breakdown (Caissie and Wilson, 1995). Pupils tell us that they understand almost nothing of what is being said during group or whole-class discussions and either become bored and resort to day dreaming or become a nuisance and seek to distract others. Part of being able to hear in a group situation is listening not only to what is being said but also attending to the social cues of taking turns. Effective communication in a group depends upon skills such as being able to locate the speaker, recognising subtle changes in conversational tone which indicate that the speaker is about to stop talking, contributing to an already established topic or initiating a new one. Contributions must also be carefully timed to ensure that they are inserted at appropriate junctures to avoid overlap with other contributions. If two speakers begin to talk simultaneously, one must stop and wait until another opportunity to talk occurs. When the speaker's turn is completed turn-yielding signals allow for the smooth exchange of turns.

In most mainstream classes pupils spend their time listening to their teachers present material orally and quickly learn that frequently a teacher-initiated question–answer routine predominates (Hopwood, 2003). Even therapeutic interventions such as speech and language therapy usually consist of one-to-one adult-directed exchanges. Deaf children, therefore, don't usually have much opportunity to develop their group communication skills and may avoid or sit passively through group discussions and consequently have less rather than more opportunity to develop their interactive skills. Without specific intervention and training in clarification techniques deaf pupils will remain inefficient and ineffective communicators. Gross (1996) emphasises that although individualised tasks are often the preferred teacher response to pupils this can deny those who most need it the opportunity to learn from social dialogue with 'more knowledgeable others', which is fundamental to human learning and development (p. 36).

Group discussions need to be carefully orchestrated in order to successfully include deaf pupils. This will involve staff being aware, first, that deaf pupils will not hear everything that is said and therefore may make comments out of context. Second, that if pupils have speech which is not fully intelligible, they may be embarrassed and hesitant about speaking aloud in class. Thirdly, that deaf pupils need to be encouraged to recognise the routines, conventions and rules by which group interaction is structured. In order to do this, the teacher will need to carefully control the discussion pace, identify each speaker in turn and summarise each contribution before moving on to the next speaker. Sebba et al. (1993) emphasise that in order for group work rather than individualised instruction to play a bigger role in schools teachers must accept that collaboration and successful interaction in its own right is a valid teaching aim.

Accessibility

Disability Discrimination Act (DDA)

If I was starting this [secondary] school again, I would want teachers to make it more accessible. I want them to do something about the environment and get rid of the noise and, like, have carpets and curtains everywhere. I would like them to welcome me and show me that they understand my problems.

Year 11 pupil

The DDA has set in law the existing moral obligation of providers to make full provision for pupils with hearing impairments and this includes schools' duties to pupils with hearing impairment. The third stage of the legislation made it an offence as of September 2005 for schools to place learners at a 'substantial disadvantage' because of a failure to modify the physical learning environment. In order to comply with the DDA in relation to deaf pupils schools may need to provide amplification equipment. It is essential to consult with individual pupils and their parents before purchasing specialist equipment. The precise kind of amplification technology needed will depend upon both the specific needs of pupils and the acoustics of the setting. Organisations such as the Royal National Institute for Deaf People (RNID) offer downloadable information. (See end of chapter for details of website).

Amplification technology

The most powerful way to enhance a deaf child's learning opportunities is to understand that the child must have appropriate 'amplification technology', i.e. hearing aids, radio aids, cochlear implant or sound field systems. Flexer (1999) explains the role of amplification technology by using a computer analogy and proposes that the primary concept is: data input precedes data processing. Flexer emphasises that a child from earliest days of life must have information/data in order to learn. Hearing is the principal way by which information enters the brain. Flexer suggests that the ears can be thought of as analogous to the computer keyboard and the brain can be compared to the computer 'hard drive'. If data is entered inaccurately, the child's brain will have incorrect information to process, just as if data was entered on a hard drive incorrectly using a malfunctioning keyboard. Although hearing aids, radio aids sound field systems and cochlear implants can all be thought of keyboards and as ways of entering acoustic information to the child's hard drive or brain, it is important to remember that they are not perfect keyboards. There will also need to be an emphasis on systematic listening and learning strategies. Amplification technology on its own does not ensure the development of an effective language base.

Early intervention

The longer a child's 'data entry' is inaccurate, the more damaging the snowballing effect will be on the overall development of the child's cognitive development. Conversely, the more intelligible and complete the data entered is, the better the opportunity the child will have to learn language that serves as a foundation for later reading and academic skills. The stimulation of 'hearing' in effect means the stimulation of brain growth. Hearing is powerful, and is the means to desired outcomes of spoken language, literacy skills and academic success. It is generally recognised that a key task for teachers of the deaf is to work with parents at the pre-school stage following diagnosis of hearing impairment (MacConville, 1989).

Sound field systems (SFS)

The installation of SFSs is now mandatory in all 'new build' schools because they have proved to be a powerful solution to the problem of noise and make a significant difference to the ability of *all* pupils to listen effectively. An SFS is a low-power public address system which amplifies the teacher's voice (usually by between 10 and 15 dB) so that they do not have to raise their voice in order to provide a clear and consistent signal to all pupils wherever they are located within the classroom. An SFS cuts through background noise, spreading sound evenly around the room and overcoming potential difficulties caused by distance, noise and reverberation. The sound level generated by the SFS is discreet so that students are not distracted by the system itself. Pupils who are hearing impaired will derive particular benefit from an SFS. An SFS consists of a microphone that is worn by the teacher which transmits the speaker's voice to a receiver amplifier that is attached to four or more speakers which are discreetly and strategically placed around the room. The SFS provides complete freedom of movement for the teacher via a wireless link.

Hearing aids

Pupils with significant degrees of hearing loss will usually be fitted with post-aural (behind the ear) digital hearing aids which can be adjusted to the requirements of different listening environments and most importantly can suppress background noise resulting in what is estimated to be a 40 per cent improvement in hearing and quality of life for users. Despite the technological advances in hearing aid technology they do not restore hearing levels to normal. Hearing aids are most useful if the levels of background noise are kept to a minimum and the speaker is close to the pupil – ideally within a metre or two. It is important for staff to be aware that pupils may regard their hearing aids as a 'coercive marker of disability' (Allan, 1999). Pupils, particularly at secondary schools, may prefer to fit in with their peers rather than wear a hearing aid. Staff should seek advice from a peripatetic teacher of the deaf to decide how to address such situations.

Radio aids

Radio aids were briefly described in the previous section. Deaf pupils who use a radio aid can tune their receiver to the same frequency as the transmitter on an sound field system described above. It is essential, if the pupil is going to benefit from wearing the radio aid, that the teacher uses the transmitter correctly. First, the teacher should turn the transmitter on at any point in the lesson (or assembly) at which the whole class is being addressed, positioning the microphone approximately 10 cm from the mouth. It is equally important that the teacher remembers to switch the transmitter off when not talking to the deaf pupil either individually or as part of a group. If the teacher does not turn off the transmitter, deaf pupils will continue to hear the teacher's voice as if the teacher were speaking directly to them. This could be either from another part of the classroom or from any part of the school, including the staffroom. It is important at the secondary stage that teachers remember to take off the transmitter at the end of the lesson so that the deaf pupil can take it to the next lesson. Class teachers will need to seek advice from a teacher of the deaf to ensure that the equipment is used effectively.

Cochlear implants

Although a cochlear implant can enhance a pupil's hearing it will not restore hearing to normal. The device provides a sensation of sound which is not the same as hearing people hear and has been described as being like 'daleks under water'. Children need time to adjust and make sense of the sensation that they receive. Although the role of the class (room) teacher is similar to that of any teacher with a deaf child, the class teacher also needs to be aware that although pupils with cochlear implants may react to even quiet sounds they may not be able to accurately interpret them. There are also safety and care factors that need to be taken into consideration and pupils with implants may be the focus of attention not just of the local peripatetic teacher of the deaf but also of a cochlear implant team. The local peripatetic teacher of the deaf will, however, probably be the person with whom staff in schools will have most regular contact. Guidelines for working with children with cochlear implants are available from the British Association of Teachers of the Deaf (BATOD) website which is listed at the end of this chapter.

Conclusion

As the children and young people whose views are included in this chapter testify deaf pupils have unique priorities that must be addressed if they are to be fully included within mainstream schools. Deafness strikes at the heart of educational endeavour as it means that information cannot always be gained reliably and effectively through speech and hearing alone. Facilitating access is a complex and multi-layered process which demands curricular modification and adaptation of teaching strategies. We learn from listening to pupils that language and social development are inextricably intertwined and that learning is to a large extent a social process. As teachers we must therefore emphasise and facilitate peer interaction as much as focus on our own interactions with learners. Children and young people who hear, or receive in other ways, the appropriate affirmations from their peers are enabled to create their own security, encouragement and problem-solving skills, co-operation with others, enjoyment and spontaneity. Accessibility for deaf children and young people means focusing attention not only on effective processes of teaching and learning but also on meaningful interpersonal interactions. *All* pupils stand to benefit.

Useful websites

www.ndcs.org.uk

www.rnid.org.uk

www.batod.org.uk

www.bioacoustics.com

www.becta.org.uk/cap

www.bda.org.uk

www.deafeatingdeafness.org

www.deafeducation.org.uk

www.ndcs.org.uk

www.royaldeaf.org.uk

www.deafcouncil.org.uk

Chapter 6

Including Pupils with Physical Disabilities

Dr Ruth M. MacConville
Stephen Dedridge

Introduction

'Physical disability' is an umbrella term that covers a whole range of physical disabilities. The child's physical difficulties turn into a disability if they prevent or disable the individual from participating in society in general and school in particular. Children who are poorly co-ordinated may be physically disabled because they are unable to complete the coursework required for examination courses; however, the same children, provided with word processors and appropriate software, may no longer be physically disabled even if they continue to have the same physical disabilities. According to the Special Educational Needs and Disability Act 2001, a young person can be described as 'physically disabled' if they have a physical impairment that has a 'substantial and long-term adverse effect on his or her ability to carry out normal day-to-day activities'.

Types of physical disability

Definition of 'physical disability'.

There are three main conditions that affect children and young people:

Muscular dystrophy (MD): affects 1 in every 3,000 children (virtually always boys). There are more than 20 different types of MD, a group of conditions that are caused by genetic damage in muscle cells. This may cause slow, progressive muscle wasting, leading to increasing difficulty in walking, clumsiness, frequent falls, difficulty standing and breathing problems. However, the symptoms and their severity vary with the different types of MD. Overall, about 1 in 2,000 babies born in the UK will have a neuromuscular disorder. Duchenne MD, the commonest and most severe form, only affects boys. Around 100 boys are born with the condition in the UK each year.

Spina bifida: affects 1 in every 300 to 1,000 (N.B. significant regional variations). Sometimes, a baby's spinal cord does not develop normally during pregnancy. When this happens, the child can have a physical disability called spina bifida. The type and amount of disability caused by spina bifida will depend upon the level of the abnormality of the spinal cord. The mildest kind of spinal bifida affects between 5% and 10% of people. In these cases there are little or no outward signs. Children with the most severe form of spina bifida may have partial or full paralysis of the legs and difficulties with bowel and bladder control. They may also have hydrocephalus (high pressure on the brain because of fluid not being drained away as normal), bone and joint deformities and curvature of the spine.

Cerebral palsy: affects 1 in every 400 children. This condition is caused by damage to the parts of the brain which control movement during the early stages of development. In most cases this damage occurs during pregnancy. However, damage can sometimes occur during birth and from brain injuries in early infancy (such as lack of oxygen from near drowning, or being shaken). Children with cerebral palsy may have difficulties with posture, movement of body parts or the whole body, muscle weakness or tightness, involuntary muscle movements, problems with balance and co-ordination, talking and eating.

In addition there are a whole range of genetic conditions (affecting 1 in every 20,000 births) that have a bearing on children's physical skills, e.g. brittle bone disease.

Acquired brain and spinal injuries are another cause of physical disability and may result from permanent injuries to the brain or limbs that prevent proper movement in parts of the body. The degree of paralysis that results from spinal injuries depends on the level of damage to the spinal cord. The higher up in the body the injury occurs, the more serious the potential paralysis can be. A paraplegic has partial or full paralysis to their lower body whereas a tetraplegic or quadriplegic is without use of their hands and arms as well.

Secondary difficulties

A number of these conditions are related directly to the developing brain, in particular cerebral palsy. This means that there may be a variety of other neurological difficulties associated with physical disabilities, particularly sensory impairment and epilepsy. Children and young people with physical disabilities may have all or none of these secondary difficulties.

In January 2005, there were 24,850 pupils in England recorded as having a physical disability and receiving special educational needs provision at School Age Plus or above, of which 80 per cent attended mainstream schools. The actual number of physically disabled pupils can be assumed to be considerably higher than this figure, as it does not include pupils who are able to access the curriculum without special educational needs provision.

Personal account

James

I was born with cerebral palsy which means the part of my brain which controls my legs doesn't work very well. I use a wheelchair. I don't think that this is the most important thing about me, as I grew up with it, but it is a big issue for other people. When my parents first approached the local primary school about me attending, they were horrified and they tried to do anything they could to stop me going to that school. A dispute with the local council who said I had to go dragged on for months and although I was only young at the time I knew that people saw me as a 'problem' and that I was 'unwanted'.

The school eventually said they would only allow me to go if I had an adult helper with me all the time. She followed me everywhere, I was unable to get rid of her. She even followed me to the toilets. She was always doing things for me even when I could do them myself. It made me feel useless like a baby. I think she was there because the teachers said I needed help, but actually it was the teachers who needed her because I think they were scared of how to cope with me on their own. One day I arrived at school and the helper wasn't there so the teacher said I would have to go back home. My mum was angry. Couldn't the teacher bear to have me in the class until the helper arrived?

As time went on it got better – people starting seeing me more as a normal person, but even during the last term in primary school something happened which made me feel really angry and for the first time stopped me feeling guilty about my disability. It made me realise that I had nothing to be ashamed of. The Year 6 were putting on a play after the end of SATs and everybody was given a role. I love acting and really thought I stood a chance of getting a good part in the play. The class teacher decided I should sit off the stage with the Year 5 children who sang songs but didn't do any of the acting. That made me really angry. I refused to go to the performance. Up until that time I had always apologised for my disability and felt guilty about it. But I realised that I had done nothing wrong and it was them who had the problem not me.

Now I am in secondary school, things are a lot better because it is a school that is designed for people with wheelchairs. I don't have too many problems apart from [the fact that] although I got a five in my English SATS I was put in the lower set and also the tables in the canteen are too low so the wheelchair users have to sit on our own table away from our mates at lunchtime.

Most of the kids treat me like I'm no different. If I do have a problem, it is with kids who don't know me. They sometimes stare at me like I'm a freak or talk to me like I'm an idiot. They speak very slowly and loudly and talk over my head. Once in a maths lesson a girl just sat there staring at me. I asked her what is her problem? She denied she was staring at me but I knew. I'm lucky I can speak because once they get to know me they realise I'm not an idiot and talk normally to me. On the whole kids treat me OK.

Adults though are far worse, because they sometimes speak to each other as if you are not in the room. They talk to each other like, 'Doesn't he use big words?' as if I should just sit there and gaggle and poo my pants. They sometimes think they are helping me but in fact they are being really annoying and patronising, which can be difficult to deal with.

On the whole things have got a lot better for kids like me. If I was born in the Roman times, I would have been thrown off a cliff or dumped in a river as soon as anybody realised that I had a disability. If I was born 50 years ago, I would have been put in a work house. If I was born 20 years ago, I might not have had the opportunity to go to a mainstream school. If I could change one thing, it would be people's attitudes.

The social challenge: what young people tell us

We need to be seen and understood so non-disabled people can relate to and accept us and understand that we want a full life like everyone else.

The following comments were made by one of the young people who took part in the 'Disability on the Box' survey which explored the attitudes of teenagers (both disabled and non-disabled) as to how disability is portrayed on the television. The survey results indicate that young people recognise the power of TV to affect the attitudes of their age group: 70 per cent of both disabled and non-disabled teenagers felt that the best way of encouraging non-disabled people to see disabled people as 'normal' is to see them regularly in mainstream TV programmes where their disability is not the focus (Whizz Kids, 2003).

It's always more pleasing to see a disabled character among non-disabled friends so that the issue isn't about their disability.

Disabled teenagers tell us that seeing disabled characters on TV has a positive effect, inspiring them and making them hopeful that negative attitudes towards disabled people will change.

They should portray disabled people in a positive, 'normal' way and show how they can contribute to society and feel valued. Also, non-disabled people can learn from disabled people and change their attitude on the whole.

Unfortunately disabled people on TV are most noticeable by their absence. Of the teenagers who took part in the Whizz Kids survey (2003), very few of them could remember seeing a disabled person in anything other than news and documentaries. Now almost three years later most teenagers would be very quick to name at least one TV character who uses a wheelchair – Andy in *Little Britain*. Yet it is a subject of debate as to whether this represents progress. *Little Britain's* Andy is a grubby, unemployed slob who fakes his disability in order to exploit his carer and turn him into his personal slave. The fact that Andy is not really physically impaired at all and is shown as able to walk, swim or even climb a tree when his carer's back is turned feeds into the traditional stereotype that people with physical impairments could 'walk if they really wanted to', are lazy and 'having us on'.

Such a negative representation of a wheelchair user would not matter and the joke could be better enjoyed if other prime time programmes included alternative, more positive representations, but generally people with physical disabilities remain invisible from our screens, reinforcing the image that they are somehow outside of 'normal' life. Even the recent promotion of disabled icon Alison Lapper, whose 16-foot-high statue by Marc Quinn currently stands in a prominent position on the fourth plinth in London's Trafalgar Square, outside the National Gallery, reinforces the view that disabled people are somehow outside the norm. It would be naïve to assume that young people and children in schools are not influenced by such images. Individuals may feel powerless to influence the national media, except perhaps to write letters of protest, but it is essential that schools provide an environment in which such representations are challenged.

Unfortunately young people tell us this is not the case. They report that they rarely see any reference to disability or images of disabled people around the school or in textbooks or worksheets. Physical disability is rarely discussed or mentioned and when it is, it is in a negative context, for example as a reason for why a woman might have an abortion.

> I can't remember disability even being talked about in lessons except for once when we read this poem in English about this boy who was teased because he had a limp.
>
> *Year 10 pupil*

> We learnt about what the Nazis did to kids if they were disabled. It was terrible. How can you gas someone to death just because they can't walk or they are very weak? It upset me but it is important to be taught about it.
>
> *Year 9 pupil*

Young people express a desire to know more about disability, especially in terms of how it affects their peers. One study in to the attitude of non-disabled pupils towards the inclusion of disabled pupils in their school showed that they:

> generally felt that their knowledge about the disabled pupils was limited and frequently used the phrase, 'I don't know what's wrong with them in relation to their disabled peers … and felt they had to 'pick up information as they went along'. One pupil felt he 'had the right to know' and another felt information was important in knowing how to treat a disabled person ... Generally [they] thought that they'd be happier about

inclusion of their disabled peers if more information were provided in school and that it was 'wrong' that knowledge had to be acquired through external sources.

(Inclusive Solutions, 2003)

Access

As well as feeling that their existence is being ignored, physically disabled young people also find it difficult to socialise with their peers because they are often unable to travel around the school at lunchtimes and breaktimes independently. Pupils tell us that doors are too heavy, corridors too narrow, lifts are too small or are broken and that there are no accessible paths across grassy areas and that playground surfaces are uneven. Therefore, the young person who wishes to be with friends at breaktimes is forced to rely on an adult or the goodwill of those peers.

> *I wish they would make it so I could get around the school with no helper. It is like having your mum with you all the time.*
>
> *Year 6 pupil*

For some schools, the solution to this problem is to set up alternative playtime arrangements. Pupils tell us that they can either stay in their classroom or go to the SEN Base at breaktimes. This can be a problem because, as Fox (2003) writes, 'playtimes and lunch-break are two obvious times when friendships can develop' (p. 118).

> *I have my lunch in the Learning Support Room. Sometimes one of the learning support assistants who are there will offer to take me out to the playground but often I spend the whole lunchtime there. Two of my friends are allowed to stay with me but no more, which is a bit awkward. When it is raining it is great because all the other kids just get wet or cold but in the summer my friends want to go outside so most times I end up on my own.*
>
> *Year 8 pupil*

Study Support

Study Support is also another area of exclusion which pupils tell us about, despite the great emphasis which has been recently placed on it by the government, who defines it as:

> learning activity outside normal lessons which young people take part in voluntarily. Study Support is, accordingly, an inclusive term, embracing many activities with many names and guises. Its purpose is to improve young people's motivation, build their self-esteem and help them to become more effective learners. Above all it aims to raise achievement'.

(DfEE, 1999)

According to a three-year study described in *The Essential Guide to the Impact of Study Support* (DfES, 2002), Study Support results in improved attendance and attitudes to school and better exam results. One might also add that it develops and extends peer relationships. In this context it is concerning that disabled people are often denied access to Study Support. Inflexible transport arrangements are one reason for this. Another reason is that the pupil may not be provided with the additional support they need (or are perceived to need) to enable them to attend. In some cases, the person managing the after-school activity will refuse to admit the disabled young person, often on the grounds of 'health and safety'.

> When I was at primary school a coach from a football team came into school to teach football skills after school. I play wheelchair football so wanted to go, but the teacher said it wasn't really suitable for me. He was very nice about it but I felt really upset.
>
> *Year 10 pupil*

A survey carried out by Eleni Burgess (2003), herself a young wheelchair user, revealed that 60% of the physically disabled teenagers who completed the survey had learnt to play a musical instrument (mostly outside school) yet only 10% of these pupils played in a school orchestra or band. As Burgess states, 'again one sees disabled pupils pursuing activities alone rather than with their classmates' (p. 3).

Physically disabled pupils tell us that they are also often excluded from school trips. Often, the school will book a coach which has no lift and no clamps for securing the wheelchair or there will be no access for wheelchairs at the chosen destination. Pupils tell us that they are left behind while their classmates enjoy themselves, and are either sent home for the duration of the trip or stay in school and join another class. Exclusion is even more likely if a trip is a 'residential' and involves travel abroad.

> I was not able to go on the last school trip because the teaching assistant who looks after me was unable to go, so I spent the day in the library.
>
> *Year 5 pupil*

> I went on a theatre trip to see 'Blood Brothers'. My drama teacher said there would be no problem and the theatre was fine. But there was no lift to get into the coach. One of the teachers carried me in his arms which made me feel so embarrassed.
>
> *Year 10 pupil*

The overall picture that many young people describe to us is of 'partial' inclusion, as they are denied full access to many of the avenues through which social relationships develop and are maintained within schools.

The social challenge: what we can do about it

If we really want to help disabled people, we could begin by simply seeing them. Society merely has first to understand that the disabled must be visible and present instead of hidden and discreet.

As disabled icon Alison Lapper (2005) writes:

> We are a disadvantaged group in society who most people find difficult to relate to. We are an awkward nuisance for most people and they usually deal with us by not dealing with us. There is a phrase which says children should be seen and not heard. I think there is a similar implicit phrase which says disabled people should be seen and not heard. And many disabled people live their lives conforming to that idea. They give into the pressures; the staring, the impatient looks and disgusted faces

(p. 8)

The difference between individuals being 'visible and present' rather than 'hidden and discreet' is in fact the difference between the medical and the social models of disability. Dr Ossie Stuart (2006, personal communication) poses the question 'So, what is disability?' and suggests that although there may appear to be an obvious answer to this question, in fact how we understand what disability is determines how we treat disabled people. Stuart emphasises that this has become all the more pertinent because the significance of the legislation protecting disabled people from discrimination, the Disability Discrimination Act of 1995 (DDA) and the 2005 Amendment, has dawned on most providers of services and employers (including schools and colleges). Ossie Stuart suggests that how well these institutions and service providers treat disabled people and meet their obligations under the law depends on their understanding of what disability is.

Two views of disability

In order to successfully include a disabled pupil it is important that staff are aware of how parents and other professionals view disability (Quinn, 1998). The 'medical model' of disability and the 'social model' of disability are different (but not competing) ways of understanding disability. When it comes to avoiding discrimination against disabled people it is the social model that has greater importance. When we think of the term 'disability' there is a list of characteristics that usually come to mind:

▸ Unable to do things for oneself

▸ Limited

▸ In need of help

▸ Malfunction of the body

use examples [handwritten annotation]

- Dis-abled
- Not able to overcome obstacles
- Not able to do all the things other people can do
- Special.

The main thing we think about when we visualise disability is the limitation it imposes on someone. In other words, what makes disabled people 'disabled' is their malfunctioning body or, in other words, their impairment. As a consequence we focus upon repairing the body, getting rid of the impairment. This is the role of the medical profession and scientists, who spend considerable time and effort try to find cures for various disabilities. The medical profession provides the name for this model because of the emphasis upon the body and their role in mitigating the worst aspects of the 'impairment'. As a consequence we tend to associate disability with negativity. For example, disabled people 'suffer' from impairment or are 'brave' because they have overcome the limitations disability imposes upon them. Many would identify the following description as a good summary of the medical model: 'Disability is ... a restraint or loss of function ... a tragedy that means dependency on others'.

The medical model versus the social model

The medical model immediately poses real challenges for providers of services and employers. How do you ensure that you do not discriminate against disabled people? Does this mean we should treat them as 'special'? Should we provide them with special services to meet their special needs? Indeed, this is the route many schools and some colleges have gone down and justified it by pointing to all the problems disabled young people face. In the opinion of many educators these are problems that can only be addressed by providing distinct services that in effect segregate disabled young people from their peers. In other words a disabled person's body is the problem, as it does not fit the way we have designed our service. This view is in complete contrast to what disability means in the social model of disability.

The medical model blames the disabled person for creating the problem for the service provider. In order to illustrate this Ossie Stuart (2006, personal communication) describes a recent experience:

> On the arrival of a black taxi cab to take me to a meeting and on seeing I was a wheelchair user, the taxi driver started to shout at me. He accused me of deceitfully not informing the company that I used a wheelchair. He was angry that he had now to take out his wheelchair ramps. This experience was deeply humiliating for me. Worse, I knew that if he had known I was a wheelchair user he would have refused to take the fare in the first place. This is despite the fact he is contractually and physically able to take my wheelchair in his taxi. Nevertheless, I was the problem

because I was unable to use the service in a way he was willing to provide it. If you blame disabled people for creating problems (or challenges) for your service, you are probably failing disabled people and possibly breaking the law. The big difference between the medical and social models is how disability is created. In the former model it is the human body that is the problem. Therefore it is understandable for that taxi driver to be inconvenienced by my inability to walk. After all, my wheelchair was too big. It might also soil his nice clean taxi and make it less pleasant for other customers. The focus is on me. I am the problem. I am to blame.

The social model takes issue with this focus on my body. First of all, we all have impairments. Whether it is short sight, long sight, or athletes foot, we all have impairments. Who we decide to call 'disabled people' is arbitrary. At one time wearing glasses was treated as a disability and pupils used to be called 'four eyes'. Now designer spectacles are coveted by most young people, wearing glasses is no longer a disability. We invent disability and how we understand disability is changing.

That incident with the taxi driver is a great example as to how much it has changed. You all probably thought that the taxi driver was rude and disrespectful. He was much more than that, he was breaking the law. If we accept that I merely have an impairment just like everybody else, then I should have been able to use the taxi service as anybody could. Why I could not had nothing to do with me but everything to do with the taxi company and the taxi driver. To put it simply they had created a barrier to me using their service. This is central to what is meant by the social model of disability. Rather than blaming me for having an impairment, it blames society (yes, including that taxi driver) for disabling me by creating barriers to me using a service.

Disability is now understood as the loss of opportunity to take part in mainstream activities due to physical or social barriers.

The real distinction between the medical and social models is where disability is produced. The social model is good news for providers of services. To avoid discriminating against disabled people you can focus on your service and whether it is creating barriers to disabled people using it. If you think you have to create a segregated special service for disabled people, it probably means your main service is failing this group of clients. Furthermore, it may mean you are breaking the law. Disabled people are not special. They are entitled to use the same service as you deliver to everybody else. If they cannot your organisation has created disability and disabling barriers and the law requires you to remove them.

Disability Discrimination Act 1995 (DDA) and the 2005 Amendment

As a result of the Disability Discrimination Act 1995 (DDA) and the 2005 Amendment it has become unlawful for schools to discriminate against disabled pupils. A school discriminates if:

▶ it treats disabled pupils less favourably than another for a reason related to their disability and without justification;

▸ it fails, without justification, to take reasonable steps to avoid placing disabled pupils at a substantial advantage. This duty is often known as the 'reasonable' adjustments' duty.

The reasonable adjustments duty requires schools to think ahead, anticipate the barriers that disabled pupils may face and remove or minimise them before a disabled pupil is placed at a substantial disadvantage. In order to avoid discrimination against any disabled pupil all staff need to implement the duties in relation to their area of responsibility: in the classroom for a teacher; on a school trip for a member of staff planning a school trip; at breaktimes and lunchtimes for ancillary staff; in a particular area of the curriculum for those with curriculum responsibilities and across the whole school for the head teacher.

Accessibility plans

All schools are legally required to develop accessibility strategies and plans to improve access to school education for disabled pupils. Access plans are required to show how, over time, schools are:

▸ increasing access to the curriculum for disabled pupils;

▸ making improvements to the physical environment of the school;

▸ making written information accessible in a range of different ways for disabled pupils.

The starting point for developing an accessibility plan should be that all children have the same provision and opportunities throughout the school day, including playtimes and lunchtimes. In some cases alternative arrangements might be necessary. For example, if a child is prone to chest infections, there may be a legitimate reason for allowing the child to stay indoors in cold weather. Yet it should not be automatically assumed, for example, that children have to stay indoors simply because they use a wheelchair. It is important to ensure that pupils in wheelchairs are not penalised by their lack of mobility or are denied 'everyday adventures' (Palmer, 2006, p. 60). These are small but significant experiences through which children and young people learn about the world. Palmer emphasises that everyday adventures are an unpredictable but essential part of growing up and are opportunities to make judgements, take risks, learn how to make friends and elude enemies. Everyday adventures, however, depend on the freedom to be 'out', not closeted at home or at school.

Because disabled children are more likely to be excluded from Study Support, their attendance needs to be carefully monitored. If disabled children are not attending Study Support, staff need to investigate the reason why. Of course disabled children should be allowed to opt out of such sessions just like any other children. It is important, however, that staff establish whether non-attendance is a genuine personal choice or whether the child has encountered obstacles that need to be addressed.

When arranging school trips, staff should be required by the senior management team to consider accessibility at the early planning stage and not just as an afterthought. To put it in context, imagine a teacher was told that the place they intended to organise a school trip to could not cater for children who were black. Would the teacher go ahead with the trip and leave the black children at school? Of course not. But this is effectively what happens to disabled children. It is important to remember that the laws regarding the discrimination against disabled children in educational settings apply not just to the classroom but to Study Support and school trips.

Positive images

Alison Lapper (2005) writes:

> I have the impression that the able-bodied majority just can't be bothered with disability. If we walk along the beach and find a stone with a hole in it, we don't look at it with revulsion simply because other stones don't have holes in them. In fact, we may be entranced by the variety of the shape that the stone with the hole has brought to our attention. However, we don't respond in that way to the human form when it varies too much from the accepted norm.

(p. 246)

Young people, both disabled and non-disabled, give us a clear message that they want schools to provide education about the nature of disability and to ensure that physically disabled people are accurately and positively represented.

> *Kids should be taught more about disability or they will grow up ignorant. It would be a good idea if kids found out about disability in lessons and there were pictures of disabled people in school books.*

Year 10 pupil

Teaching staff need to consider ways of introducing positive images of disabled people, within school, perhaps starting with posters and displays. One useful strategy is to start to collect clippings from magazines and newspapers. Local and national organisations that cater for disabled people can help with providing resources. A recent poster campaign by the charity Changing Faces recently depicted people with a range of facial disfigurements and encouraged observers to engage with them in everyday social interactions, with messages including 'If you can hold my gaze, we could have a conversation'. This award-winning campaign was notable for two reasons. First it consisted of positive images of people with facial disfigurements and, secondly, it suggested strategies for how people who are unused to meeting others with a visible difference should act in such circumstances. It seems that this advice is needed – a YouGov (2003) opinion poll commissioned by Changing Faces found that 79 per cent of respondents would be scared of doing the wrong thing if they met someone with a severe facial disfigurement. It is important not to simply display 'charity' posters as this can reinforce the idea of disabled people as being dependent and vulnerable. Ideally disabled people should be shown participating in a range of activities and expressing a variety of emotions both positive and negative. It is also important to avoid showing disabled people just by themselves but to emphasise their everyday relationships with friends, family and work colleagues. The portrayal of people with physical difficulties as having the same personal characteristics as everyone else, good and bad, is an important message to promote in the classroom. Using a range of opportunities to provide disabled role models (both children and adults) can boost the self-esteem of disabled pupils and have a positive effect upon all pupils. This can be supported by using positive images of disabled children and adults in pictures, books and in a range of materials throughout the school (DfES, 2006).

Positive role models

Inviting disabled adults to visit schools and talk to pupils about their experiences can also help raise awareness.

> This man came to our school to talk to us about being in a wheelchair. He had to go to a special school and he was bullied a lot. He should have been able to go to a normal school.
>
> *Year 5 pupil (non-disabled)*

Every Child Matters

The government's programme of change, 'Every Child Matters' (DfES, 2003), emphasises five outcomes for children and young people which include 'the importance of making a positive contribution to the community' (para. 2.4. p. 9). For pupils with disabilities this has a particular significance and means developing their ability to express their views in the knowledge and confidence that their 'voice' will be heard (Cheminais, 2005). This is important as non-disabled children need to be provided with accurate information about their disabled classmates and ideally this information should come from disabled young people themselves. As Alison Lapper (2005) writes, 'unless people with impairments are willing to share what it's like to live our lives, the rest of the population will never be able to appreciate the difficulties we face. How can we acuse people of having no understanding of disability and then refuse to tell them anything about it?' (p. 9). As they get older children should be encouraged to talk about their disability to others. Initiatives such as the 'Powerful Voices' conference for children (MacConville, 2006a) include talks by young people with disabilities which can be used to encourage other young people to talk about their disability. Talking openly about one's disability is a very sensitive process so it is essential that each pupil is allowed to manage this at their own rate and in their own way. Some pupils will be willing to talk to a small group while other pupils may feel able to give a talk to the class. Alternatively a familiar adult can help the disabled pupil to write down information which is then read on the pupil's behalf.

If a class have been together from the start of primary school, it can often be assumed that the non-disabled children 'accept' the disabled children and it is not an issue that needs to be addressed. Nevertheless, as children grow up it is important that they are provided with more age appropriate, accurate information about the nature of their classmate's disability.

In discussing a pupil's physical impairments, staff need to use sensitivity but also be aware that the more adults treat a disability as a 'taboo' subject, the more they reinforce the idea that it is something to be ashamed about. The reality is that children and young people are not politically correct and like straightforward answers to their questions (MacConville, 2006b). Children and young people should be encouraged to treat each other with respect and also should not be afraid to ask questions. Schools are more likely to make effective, reasonable adjustments where there are strong consultative mechanisms in place for all pupils and where peer support is well developed (DfES, 2006).

> One of the boys I went to primary school with was chatting with me one day and said that his mum told him he should be nice to me because I was very ill and probably die soon. He told everyone else in his class. No wonder I got invited to all their birthday parties. They must have been watching me, expecting I would choke on the jelly and fall down dead at any moment.
>
> *Year 11 pupil*

Peer power

Learning is, to a large degree, a social process and within any classroom, the pupils represent a rich source of experiences, inspiration, challenge and support which, if utilised, can inject an enormous supply of additional energy into the tasks and activities that are set. Pupils have the capacity to contribute to one another's learning and should be encouraged to support each other. Activities such as peer mediation, peer mentoring and paired reading may be appropriate; however, it is important that *all* pupils are encouraged to develop effective team-working skills.

The more accurate information pupils have about their disabled peers and the more they are included in every aspect of school life, the less likelihood there is that teasing and bullying will occur. Nevertheless, schools need to have an effective policy and consistent and robust procedures firmly in place for dealing with bullying, and prevention measures such as peer support in place. The school's policy on bullying should make specific reference to the unacceptability of bullying pupils because of their disabilities. Children need to be educated as to why derogatory terms related to disability are both upsetting and offensive.

The learning environment: what young people tell us

When teaching staff first know that there will be a physically disabled child coming to the school, a natural reaction is to worry and ask the question, 'How will the pupil cope and how will I cope?' It is important that staff realise that such an attitude is largely based on an able-bodied view that physical disability is a problem for the pupil. It is also an aspect of the medical model of disability referred to earlier in this chapter. The focus is on how the individual pupil deviates from the 'normal', i.e. the able bodied, pupil. This can be contrasted with the social model of disability which considers that the pupil's main problem is the attitude of others and a lack of resources, i.e. the lack of facilities at the school or the attitude of their teachers. It is important that teachers do not make negative assumptions about the psychological or emotional well-being of their pupils. In fact some social psychologists assert that having a physical disability may actually provide psychological strength and motivation rather than being psychologically damaging (Crocker and Major, 1989). Alison Lapper (2005) writes:

> I have been driven by the idea that my life can be as full as anyone else's, no matter what other people think. In fact it has been precisely those times when people told me that I couldn't do something that I became the most determined to prove them wrong. The only difference for me is that I have always known that I would have to work harder than able-bodied people to achieve what I wanted. And one of the biggest obstacles to my progress has been their prejudice and limited view of what I could achieve.

> (p. 9).

Some staff are concerned about doing or saying the wrong thing and unintentionally causing hurt and offence. This can result in teaching staff feeling unsure and unskilled. There may be a well-meaning tendency to provide lots of help and support for the child. A teaching assistant assigned to a child may in particular feel that it is their responsibility to offer as much help as they can. In younger children this can create high levels of dependency and in older pupils a feeling of resentment at being treated like a baby. Another danger is that adults might give the child excessive praise for doing things which are taken for granted in other children and may not even be related to the child's physical impairments. This can make the child feel that adults have low expectations of them and that their intelligence and abilities are not respected.

> There was this French teacher who every time I answered a question would go mad like I was the cleverest person in the whole world. 'Très bien!' she would shout over and over again. She didn't do this with anybody else. She seemed amazed that I could even speak. It was so bad, the other kids noticed and used to shout, 'Très bien', at me all the time.

> *Year 9 pupil*

I think it is more difficult for some teachers than it is for me. I just get on with things but some teachers seem scared that I am going to hurt myself or that I will get upset. They can worry so much I start getting nervous myself.

Year 8 pupil

Insidious prejudice

At a conference organised by Scope, the charity for cerebral palsy, in March 2006, a young comedian called Laurence Clark told how difficult it had been at his school to get across to his carers that he was intellectually competent. That achieved, he was urged in to computing so that he could 'work at home, never go out, and make loads of money'. By the time he got his doctorate he realised that he was 'an out-going, gregarious person trapped in the body of a computer scientist' and started doing comedy instead. 'For the disabled', Clark asserts, 'computing is the new basket weaving'. The assumption that was being made by professionals on Clark's behalf was that he would see the sense in suppressing his social needs in order to 'fit in' without troubling anyone. Their attitude represents an insidious kind of prejudice because the professionals involved believed that they were acting for the best. What Clark describes is a recurring problem, whereby professionals assume that disability confers a desire to be invisible.

Appearance as our personal billboard

Our external appearance has been described as our personal billboard, providing others with information on which they base their first and sometimes only impressions (Garner, 1997). Although the external image offers in reality only a 'mere sliver' of who we are, people read a whole personality into the way we present ourselves. Goffman (1963), in his classic work on individuals with 'disfigurements', maintained that when 'normals' (his word) meet such a person they may be uncomfortable because the 'stigmatising' feature is unusual and they lack the experience to guide their behaviour and will be anxious not to behave inappropriately. A wheelchair sends a strong message of impairment, close connections with the medical profession and the signal, 'I can't walk'. Pupils tell us that their appearance evokes uncertain responses from their peers.

Sometimes I can feel very powerful in my wheelchair. I'm in the playground and I want to get over to the science block. As I move through the crowds of kids they move away from me – it's like Moses and the parting waters. That can make me feel very powerful but at the same time nobody says a word to me or even looks at me.

Year 9 pupil

Stereotypical judgements of people's attributes are also made on the basis of their appearance and pupils in wheelchairs tell us that they are often complimented and called 'brave' or 'amazing' by members of staff. Pupils tell us that they are frequently complimented for everyday acts and this can make them feel very angry.

> *I was coming up the ramp into the town hall and I got stuck in the doorway. A security guard helped me through and then he said to me, 'Well done'. Think about it – I got complimented for getting through a door.*
>
> *Year 10 pupil*

> *I went to Tesco's with my sister and at the check-out the assistant said to her, 'You are doing such a good job'. I felt so patronised and humiliated.*
>
> *Year 11 pupil*

In a recent BBC poll the word 'brave' was identified as more offensive to disabled people than 'cripple' or 'handicapped'.

The relationship between a teaching assistant and a pupil can sometimes be difficult because it can easily develop into a relationship of dependency. There can be a danger that the teaching assistant can become over-protective and attach themselves 'like Velcro' to the pupil. This does not enable the pupil to develop confidence and competency and may lead to what is termed 'learned helplessness' and even greater problems when an additional adult is not available. In some cases, the pupil may even be sent home if the teaching assistant is absent and whether or not a pupil can take part in the trip is dependent on whether the teaching assistant is willing to accompany the pupil. There can be particular issues when a teaching assistant works with a child over a period of years as it may be difficult for the teaching assistant to adapt to the child becoming older.

> *My helper used to do everything for me and I just used to sit back. I thought it was great. When I think back, I know it was wrong and I would have learnt more if she had made me do more.*
>
> *Year 12 pupil*

> *I had this really great helper in infant school but when I moved to the juniors this woman took over who fussed over me all the time and kept nagging me. She never left me alone. She was a nice lady but I hated her. My mum and dad though thought she was wonderful and even tried to get her to carry on working with me in high school. I didn't say anything because I didn't want to appear ungrateful. Luckily she didn't come with me. The teaching assistants here are much better and don't treat me like a baby.*
>
> *Year 10 pupil*

A dependency between a teaching assistant and a pupil can impede the development of a relationship between the pupil and the teacher. Some teachers encourage this by 'handing over' responsibility for the child to the teaching assistant.

My assistant always comes over and tries to help me. He doesn't always know what he is talking about and I would prefer the teacher to help me but if I tell the teaching assistant I want the teacher to help and not him, he gets angry.

Year 8 pupil

How they are supported in class and who supports them is often one of a number of decisions over which physically disabled young people tell us that they have no control. Pupils report that their opinion about their need for support is not sought or is done in a way which lacks sensitivity. For example, the person who is asked to find out what a pupil thinks about support in class is frequently the same person who provides the support! This is hardly going to encourage an honest response.

When I was younger I used to say what people wanted to hear. I always thought I should appear grateful and I think I was scared if I didn't say the right thing, they would take it out on me in some way. I guess I am a lot more stroppy now!

Year 12 pupil

Problems of access and lack of specialist equipment can also force the child to rely on adult support. The impact on social relationships of not been able to attend trips has already been noted, but this can also have an impact on learning when coursework or further lessons in class relate to a trip a child was excluded from attending. In the survey carried out by Burgess (2003), Geography was the subject where this was a significant issue.

Physical Education

Another subject from which young people are most likely to be excluded is PE. Children who enjoy sport outside school can often find themselves spending lessons watching from the sidelines.

At the beginning of Year 7, I was promised by Miss [teacher] for something different to do during PE because I could not participate in normal activities as other people do. But nothing happened. Due to this I was unable to take part in PE or any activity at all. I was just told to stand outside the gym. Other children then used this as a reason to pick on me. I reported this but the attitude was 'Now what's wrong?' I was also bullied for wearing a wig. Some pupils even tried to pull my wig off outside the gym. Even though I reported this, nothing happened. No action towards those pupils was taken. School never took my physical needs seriously. Because no care and support was given to me I became a victim of bullying which increased my anxiety leading to my fainting.

Year 8 pupil

Burgess (2003) found that 70% of the physically disabled teenagers she interviewed did sports outside school but only 30% were included in PE lessons.

Teachers often assume that pupils with physical disabilities can't do physical activities and they do not know how to organise integrated games or alternatives activities. Teachers also express concern about 'health and safety' issues relating to individual pupils' health.

> I play a lot of sports outside school – basketball, swimming and football – but my PE teacher seems to think I can't do anything.
>
> *Year 7 pupil*

Personal, Social and Health Education (PSHE)

Another area of concern is sex education. Physically disabled people are very rarely represented as having sexual feelings, sexual needs and sexual capabilities and traditionally physical disability has been associated with impotency. Fear of exploitation or pregnancy may encourage adults to either avoid talking to disabled young people about sex or presenting it in negative terms. There can also be a tendency to treat a disabled youngster as an eternal child. Research carried out among disabled teenage girls by the Disabled Women's Sexuality Project found that almost 40 per cent of interviewees stated that their parents and teachers did not expect them to form relationships, be partners or parents when they grew up (Baker, 2004).

The current PSHE curriculum may fail to give specific information about disability and sexuality and encourage the perception that relationships are only for people who are physically able. (In fact it is very unlikely that any child can identify with the 'perfect' bodies which are often drawn to show changes during puberty.) Burgess (2003) found that a significant number of disabled children did not find the information given to them in sex education lessons appropriate to them and did not feel they had an opportunity to raise questions that mattered to them within school.

The learning environment: what we can do about it

Even in the twenty-first century people are generally uncomfortable when they see a disabled person (Lapper, 2005, p. 3). Schools offer both an educational and a social environment in which to challenge attitudes and myths about disability and appearance. This is important because physical disability is frequently a trigger for bullying and teasing in schools (Crozier and Dimmock, 1999; Thomson *et al.*, 2001). Schools also offer an opportunity to include pupils with physical disabilities thus enabling both peers and staff to interact with those with disabilities and therefore encourage a greater appreciation of diversity and difference.

Proactive interventions

Despite the prevalence of appearance concerns among children and especially adolescents there are very few interventions which are specifically aimed at addressing this issue. The 'Changing Faces' approach aims to educate secondary pupils about visible difference, challenge appearance-related myths and enable pupils to generate strategies to tackle their own social difficulties. These strategies include:

▸ devising and practising a positive self-motto;

▸ preparing an explanation for their perceived difference that would reassure other people;

▸ taking charge of a conversation by responding neutrally to any teasing or bullying comments;

▸ making use of friends.

Such proactive interventions are only likely to be put in place if staff are convinced of the magnitude and impact of appearance-related concerns among adolescents. Results, however, can include improvements in pupils' body image, self-esteem and social confidence. In our experience one of the benefits of this approach is the ease with which materials can be used by staff so that specialist advisory input is not necessary once the group has been established in the school.

Understanding the medical condition

Children and young people's physical difficulties stem from different conditions and it is helpful for staff to know the medical diagnosis of their pupils. There can be significant differences between the education of a pupil with cerebral palsy and a pupil with, for example, muscular dystrophy. Understanding the medical condition is important because it enables the teacher to:

▸ liaise with other professionals who will also use the terminology;

▸ discuss issues with the parent;

▸ understand the implications of the condition;

▸ be aware of secondary problems, for example sensory impairment or tiredness.

However, every child with the same medical diagnosis does not have the same educational needs. Teachers need to understand the implications of the medical diagnosis and then understand the details of the diagnosis for each individual pupil.

Trusting relationships

In order to successfully include a physically disabled pupil, staff need to build a trusting relationship with the pupil. Even if staff have previously worked with another child with the same medical condition it is important to remember that each pupil is an individual and that with each individual we enter into a new learning experience, in which we are required to rid ourselves of previous expectations and prejudices. Egan (1990) writes that there are three critical aspects to a good relationship: respect, genuineness and empathy. The pupil needs to be treated in the same way as all other pupils with teachers showing them respect, genuineness and empathy. Fox (2003) writes that crucial for developing this interactional style is the need for staff to get to know the pupil by:

▸ exploring the pupil's interests;

▸ being positive;

▸ building on any communication.

Developing the pupil's ability to interact involves two people, the pupil and the adult. The problem is that the pupil will interact and initiate less over time unless the adult provides the motivation for the pupil to communicate.

(Fox, 2003, p. 86)

Personalised learning

The Every Child Matters agenda (DfES, 2003) emphasises personalised learning. The purpose of personalised learning is to promote personal development through self-realisation, self-enhancement and self-development. If pupils are to be an active, responsible and self-motivated learners, then they need to be encouraged to identify their own style of learning and become solution-focused in order to ensure that they become active participants in their own education. As pupils get older, it is often helpful to think of this in terms of a contract between the teacher and the pupil (and where appropriate support staff). A contract is a way of setting clear, realistic targets and agreeing the strategies for reaching the targets. They encourage careful planning and enable work to be evaluated. Contracts can empower both staff and pupils because they enable successes to be shared and realistic objectives for change to be created (MacConville, 1991). An important element of a contract is identifying what signal the pupil will use to alert staff when they need support, when they are able to work independently or when they need a rest. Establishing a 'code' can avoid embarrassing the pupil in front of others.

Personal Passports

Within a high school it is helpful if pupils (especially those with communication difficulties) create their own Personal Passport. A Personal

Passport is a document that provides key information about what is needed to enable the pupil to communicate (CALL, 1997). Personal Passports have a number of key features: information is presented in the first person and in an empowering way, emphasising the pupil's uniqueness and individuality. They are written in a succinct and selective style, emphasising what others need to know.

Personal Passports are useful when the child is starting in a new situation. They provide a focus for the teacher and TA to discuss with the parents the most important aspects of including the pupil – communication, physical needs and independence. It may also lead to changes in attitudes and an increase in confidence by the staff as they get to know the parents better. Personal Passports are particularly helpful in high schools and should be distributed to all staff. Teachers should also, however, make the effort to take the child aside and briefly discuss the passport with them. Young people are the true experts in understanding their own bodies and we need to guard against the common trap of blaming the disabled person, of assuming they could do it if they really tried hard enough.

I really like it if a teacher takes time to talk to me and find out what I think I am able to do by myself and where I think I may need help.

Year 9 pupil

It is also important that a culture is created in which teaching assistants are encouraged to feel positive the more a child does things by themselves and needs adult support less, rather than thinking that other adults will perceive them as not doing their job properly if they are not constantly helping the child.

Teaching assistants who provide personal care for a child should be shadowed by another member of staff who can take over these duties when the teaching assistant is away. It may be a good idea for more than one teaching assistant to provide support for the same pupil and adults should guard against using language which reinforces dependency, e.g. 'your helper'.

I prefer it if adults let me have a go at things first and only step in if I ask.

Year 10 pupil

We also need to challenge the traditional idea that provision for physically disabled children always means 'an extra adult'. If a child needs an adult to get into the drama studio because of a set of steps, building a ramp may not only be a preferred alternative to additional adult assistance but actually may work out as a cheaper alternative. Specialist equipment, software or making minor alterations can often significantly increase a child's independence. The research shows that there are issues that need to be addressed within specific curriculum areas. The arrangements for Geography field trips need to be reviewed as this appears to be the most common 'exam-related' experience from which physically disabled children are likely to be excluded (Burgess, 2003).

For pupils with physical disabilities there is clearly an issue with PE Teachers in this curriculum area need better training and resources need to be devoted to specialist equipment so that there are more opportunities for integrated activities. The assumption that this is the best time to do a child's physiotherapy also needs to be challenged as physiotherapy is not the same as PE or games lessons. Finally, those responsible for PSHE need to review the policy and provision to ensure that it addresses the experiences and needs of disabled youngsters.

Conclusion

The barriers that can prevent disabled pupils from being fully included in schools and playing their full part in society can be grouped into three main forms: environmental, organisational and attitudinal. Environmental barriers prevent the free movement of disabled pupils around the school and playground and jeopardise equal access to services such at Study Support or school trips. Organisational or institutional barriers are created when decisions and policy making ignore or forget the needs of disabled pupils because they are designed for the 'smooth running' of the school and are unthinkingly applied. Attitudinal barriers arise from the way disabled pupils are viewed or treated by other people. This may arise from prejudice, ignorance, lack of education, fear, lack of confidence, indifference and so on. People fail to see the disabled person as an individual, but 'put a label on them', make assumptions about disabled people, act on stereotypes, fail to treat disabled people equally and go along with the 'society of perfection'.

Campaigners for inclusion say there is no child who cannot be taught in a mainstream school if enough resources are put into the system. Richard Rieser, director of Disability Equality in Education and a member of the 2020 Campaign against special schools, emphasises that special schools do not work for academic achievement, they do not work for self-esteem and they do not work on a social level. Rieser's views are shared by many. Even charities such as Scope that run special schools believe that with enough investment the vast majority of children could go to a mainstream school. Michelle Daley, 34, is a wheelchair user who bitterly regrets the fact that she went to a special school. 'I don't think that we should single out children,' she said. 'Parents think they are protecting their children but you have to go into the real world when you are 16' (Asthana, 2006).

When many people think about inclusion of physically disabled children and young people they think about ramps and lifts and 'disabled toilets'. Physical access is without doubt an important issue and pupils inform us that inadequate access can impact on social relationships and on learning. Yet listening to children and young people emphasises for us that making changes in buildings and providing specialist equipment is just the beginning. What is most important are attitudes and the refusal by teaching staff to continue to be party to the discrimination of young people because of their physical impairment. Non-disabled adults do not know what it is like to be physically disabled within their school. They can only find out by listening.

Useful websites

www.scope.org.uk

www.iCerebralPalsy.info

www.muscular-dystrophy.org

www.mda.org

www.strategy.gov.uk/work_areas/disability/index.asp

www.mailbase.ac.uk/lists/disability-research/files.children.rtf

www.ifglobal.org/home.asp

www.ssba.org.uk

www.inclusive_solutions.com/childrensattitudestoinclusion.asp

Conclusion

During the past two decades there has been an accelerating movement towards ideas about children and young people's participation and voice. Enshrined in Article 12 of the United Nations Convention on the Rights of the Child, these notions have gathered both support and efforts at practical implementation. Thus, the views of children and young people are beginning to find their way into many of the forums of the adult world and challenge us to reconsider the ways in which we engage with the discourse of inclusion. We want this book to accelerate that process. We believe that the emergence of children's voice and their participation can colour and inform adult perspectives in the service of honesty and improved services and that without the active participation of young people there will be no social future.

In the process of writing this book we have learnt some of the ways that we can enable children and young people to be involved in a dialogue with us. The first is to accept that all children have the right to be included. The second is to look actively for children's competence and engage with where they are 'coming from'. The third is to use ways of communicating that children find helpful and engaging, especially humour. The fourth is to give children sufficient time to express their views in their own way. The last is to treat children, and their views, with respect. At the heart of the approach that we have offered here is a commitment to positive relationships. Listening to children and young people offers us the opportunity to reconsider our ways of relating to young people and reflect on the messages that we convey in our everyday interactions.

We believe that we have to continue to find means of listening more effectively to children and young people and particularly, as this book has emphasised, those who are vunerable. An emphasis on the quality of relationships is frequently sufficient to empower pupils to take a more active role in their own well-being.

It leaves me to thank all the children and young people who have contributed their thoughts and ideas to create the spirit of this book. Without their words this book could not have been written.

Dr Ruth M. MacConville

References

Ainscow, M. (1999) *Understanding the Development of Inclusive Schools*, London: Falmer Press

Allan, J. (1999) *Actively Seeking Inclusion: Pupils with Special Needs in Mainstream Schools*, London: Falmer Press

Anderson, C. W. (1994) 'Teaching the subject matter to students who struggle with reading, writing and spelling'. Presented at the annual conference of the National Orton Dyslexia Society, November, Los Angeles, CA

Arter, C., Mason, H., McCall, S., McLinden, M. and Stone, J. (1999) *Children with Visual Impairment in Mainstream Settings*, London: David Fulton Publishers

Asthana, A. (2006) 'Meet James and Joshua: too difficult to teach in school?', *The Observer*, 14 May

Attwood, T. (2004), *Exploring Feelings: Cognitive Behaviour Therapy to Manage Anger.* Arlington, TX: Future Horizons

Baker, S. (2004), *Sex and Relationship Education for Young people with Physical Disabilities: A Booklet for Teachers*, London: Contact a Family Publications

Baron-Cohen, S., Tager-Flusberg, H. and Chen, D. (2000) *Understanding Other Minds: Perspectives from Developmental Cognitive Neuroscience*, Oxford: Oxford University Press

Barratt, P. and Thomas, B. (1999) 'The inclusion of students with Asperger syndrome in a mainstream secondary school: a case study', *Good Autism Practice*, September, pp. 65–71

Barrow, G., Bradshaw, E. and Newton, T. (2001) *Improving Behaviour and Raising Self-esteem in the Classroom: A Practical Guide to Using Transactional Analysis,* London: David Fulton Publishers

Barrow, G. and Newton, T. (2004), *Walking the Talk*, London: David Fulton Publishers

Bathurst, B. (2005) 'Focus: living with deafness. How I learnt to love my silent world', *The Observer*, 23 January, p. 20

Bauman, M. K. (1964) 'Group differences disclosed by inventory items', *International Journal for Education of the Blind*, 13, pp. 101–6

Bayliss, N. (2005) *Learning from Wonderful Lives*, Cambridge: Cambridge Well-Being Books

BDA (British Dyslexia Association) (2005) *Achieving Dyslexia Friendly Schools: Resource Pack*, London: British Dyslexia Association

Bettelheim, B. and Zelan, K. (1982) *On Learning to Read: The Child's Fascination with Meaning*, New York: Vintage Books

Bienvenu, M. (1985) *An Introduction to American Deaf Culture*, Silver Springs, MD: Sign Media Inc.

Burgess, E. (2003) *Are We Nearly There Yet?: Do Teenage Wheelchair Users Think Integration has been Achieved in Secondary Schools in the UK?* Project sponsored by Whizz Kids No Limits, Millenium Awards

CALL (Communication Aids for Language and Learning) (1997) *Personal Passports*, Edinburgh: CALL

Caissie, R. and Wilson, E. (1995) 'Communication breakdown management during co-operative learning activities by mainstreamed students with hearing losses', *Volta Review*, 97, pp. 105–21

Cassar, M., Treiman, R., Moats, L., Pollo, T. C. and Kessler, B. (2005) 'How do spellings of children with dyslexia compare with those of nondyslexic children?', *Reading and Writing*, 18, pp. 27–49

Chalk, M. and Smith, H. (1995) 'Training professionals to run social skills groups for children', *Educational Psychology in Practice*, 11:2, pp. 30–6

Cheminais, R. (2005) *Every Child Matters: A New Guide for SENCOs*, London: David Fulton Publishers

Clarke, J. I. and Dawson, C. (1998) *Growing Up Again*, Minnesota, MN: Hazleden

Clunies-Ross, L. and Franklin, A. (eds) (1997) 'Where have all the children gone?', *British Journal of Visual Impairment*, 15, pp. 48–52

Cooper, P., Smith, C. J. and Upton, G. (1994) *Emotional and Behavioural Difficulties: Theory to Practice*, London: Routledge

Coppock, C. and Dwivedi, K. N. (1993) 'Group work in schools', in Dwivedi, K. N. (ed.) *Group Work with Children and Adolescents: A Handbook*, London: Jessica Kingsley Publishing

Corbett, J. (2002) 'Inclusion', *Special Children*, 146, pp. 14–17

Corker, M. (1994) *Counselling*, London: Jessica Kingsley Publishing

Corley, G., Robinson, D. and Lockett, S. (1989) *Partially Sighted Children*, London: NFER-Nelson

Cowie, H. and Wallace, P. (2000) *Peer Support in Action: From Bystanding to Standing By*, London: Sage Publications

Crocker, J. and Major, B. (1989) 'Social stigma and self-esteem: the self-protective properties of stigma', *Psychological Review*, 96:4, pp. 608–30

Crozier, W. R. and Dimmock, P. S. (1999) 'Name-calling and nicknames in a sample of primary school children', *British Journal of Educational Psychology*, 69, pp. 505–16

Davis, P. and Hopwood, V. (2002) 'Including children with a visual impairment in the mainstream primary classroom', *Journal of Research in Special Educational Needs*, 2: 3, pp. 1–11.

DES (Department of Education and Science) (1978) *Special Educational Needs* (The Warnock Report), London: HMSO

DfEE (Department for Education and Employment) (1999) *Extending Opportunity: A National Framework for Study Support*, London: HMSO

DfES (Department for Education and Skills) (2002) *The Essential Guide to the Impact of the Study Support* (Ref.: 0248/2002), Nottingham: DfES Publications Centre

DfES (Department for Education and Skills) (2003) *Every Child Matters*, London: DfES Skills

DfES (Department for Education and Skills) (2004) *Removing Barriers to Achievement: The Government's Strategy for SEN*, London: DfES

DfES (Department for Education and Skills) (2006) *Implementing the Disability Discrimination Act in Schools and Early Years Settings*, London: DfES

Dunlea, A. (1989) *Vision and the Emergence of Meaning: Blind and Sighted Children's Early Language*, Cambridge: Cambridge University Press

Egan, G. (1990) *The Skilled Helper* (4th edn), Monterey, CA: Brooks-Cole

Elliott, J. (2005) 'Dyslexia, diagnoses, debates and diatribes', *Special Children*, November/December, pp. 19–23.

Elliott, J. (2006) 'Coming to terms with dyslexia', *Special*, Spring, pp. 35–7

Fletcher, L. (1987) *A Language for Ben: A Child's Right to Sign*, London: Souvenir Press

Flexer, C. (1999) *Facilitating Hearing and Listening in Young Children*, San Diego, CA: Singular Publishing

Fox, M. (2003) *Including Children 3–11 with Physical Disabilities*, London: David Fulton Publishers

Frances, J. (2004) *Educating Children with Facial Disfigurement: Creating Inclusive School Communities*, London: Routledge Falmer

Frank, R. and Livingston, K. E. (2003) *The Secret Life of the Dyslexic Child*, London: Rodale International

Gallaway, C. (1998) 'Early interaction', in Gregory, S., Knight, P., McCracken, W., Powers, S. and Watson, L. (eds) *Issues in Deaf Education*, London: David Fulton Publishers

Garner, D. M. (1997) 'The 1997 body image survey results', *Psychology Today*, 30, pp. 30–4, 75–80, 84

Gersch, I. (2000) 'Listening to children: an initiative to increase the active involvement of children in their education by an educational psychology service', in *Professional Development for Special Educational Needs Co-ordinators*, Milton Keynes: Open University Press

Goffman, E. (1963) *Stigma: Notes on the Management of a Spoiled Identity*, Englewood Cliffs, NJ: Prentice Hall

Goldstein, E. (1999) *Sensation and Perception*, Pacific Grove, CA: Brooks/Cole

Goleman, D. (1996) *Emotional Intelligence*, London: Bloomsbury

Grandin, T. (1995) *Thinking in Pictures and Other Reports on My Life with Autism*. New York: Bantam

Gray, C. (1999) *Teaching Social Understanding with Social Stories and Comic Strip Conversations*, Jenison, MI: Jenison Public Schools

Gray, C. D., Hosie, J. A., Russell, P. A. and Ormel, E. A. (2001) 'Emotion Development in deaf children: facial expressions, display rules and theory of mind', in Clark, M. D., Marschark, M. and Karchmer, M. (eds) *Context, Cognition and Deafness*, Washington, DC: Gallaudet University Press

Greenberg, M. T. and Kusche, C. (1993) *Promoting Social and Emotional Development in Deaf Children: The Paths Project*, Seattle, WA: University of Washington Press

Greenhalg, R. (1994) *Emotional Growth and Learning*, London: Routledge

Greenhalg, P. (1996) 'Behaviour: roles, responsibilities and referrals in the shadow of the Code of Practice', *Support for Learning*, 11:1, pp. 17–24

Gregory, S. and Hartley, G. M. (1994) *Constructing Deafness*, Milton Keynes: Open University Press

Gregory, S. and Knight, P. (1998) 'Social development and family life', in Gregory, S., Knight, P., McCracken, W., Powers, S. and Watson, L. (eds) *Issues in Deaf Education*, London: David Fulton Publishers

Gross, J. (1996) *Special Educational Needs in the Primary School: A Practical Guide*, Buckingham: Open University Press

Gross, J. and White, A. (2003) *Special Educational Needs and School Improvement*, London: David Fulton Publishers

Hannah, L. (2001) *Teaching Young Children with Autistic Spectrum Disorders to Learn: A Practical Guide for Parents and Staff in Mainstream Schools and Nurseries*, London: The National Autistic Society

Happe, F. (1994) *Autism: An Introduction to Psychogical Theory*, London, UCL Press

Hargreaves, A. (1994) *Changing Teachers, Changing Times*, London: Cassell

Harrell, R. L. and Strauss, F. A. (1986) 'Approaches to increasing assertive behaviour and communication skills in blind and visually impaired persons', *Journal of Visual Impairment and Blindness*, June, pp. 794–8

Harris, J. R. (1998) *The Nurture Assumption*, New York: Free Press

Hart, S. (1996) *Beyond Special Needs*, London: Paul Chapman Publishing

Hartup, W. W. (1996) 'Cooperation, close relationships and cognitive development', in Bukowski, W. M., Newcomb, A. F. and Hartup, W. W. (eds) *The Company They Keep: Friendship in Childhood and Adolescence*, Cambridge: Cambridge University Press

Hindley, P. A., Hill, P. D., McGuian, S. and Kitson, N. (1994) 'Psychiatric disorder in deaf and hearing impaired children and young people: a prevalence study', *Journal of Child Psychology and Psychiatry*, 35, pp. 917–34

Hindley, P. A. and Reed, H. (1999) 'Promoting Alternative Thinking Strategies (PATHS): mental health promotion with deaf children in school', In Decker, S., Kirby, S., Greenwood, A. and Moore, D. (eds) *Taking Children Seriously: Applications of Counselling and Therapy in Education*, London: Cassell

Hopwood, V. (2003) 'Deaf children in hearing classrooms: teacher–pupil talk in secondary schools', in Gallaway, C. and Young, A. (eds) *Deafness and Education in the UK: Research Perspectives*, London: Whurr Publishers

Howlin, P., Baron-Cohen, S. and Hadwin, J. (1999) *Teaching Children with Autism to Mind-Read*, Chichester: John Wiley and Sons

Humphrey, N. (2002) 'Teacher and pupil ratings of self-esteem in developmental dyslexia', *British Journal of Special Education*, 29:1, pp. 29–36

Humphrey, N. and Mullins, P. (2002) 'Personal constructs and attribution for academic success and failure in dyslexia', *British Journal of Special Education*, 29:4, pp. 196–203

Hutchinson, J. (2006) 'It's a boy's world', *Junior Magazine*, August, pp. 39–42

Inclusive Solutions (2003) *Children's Attitudes Towards Inclusion: A Study Investigating Children's Attitudes towards the Inclusion of a Young Disabled Person into a Mainstream Class*. Available from: www.inclusivesolutions.com/childrensattitudesto inclusion.asp (accessed June 2005)

Jones, G. (2002) *Educational Provision for Children with Autism and Aspergers Syndrome*, London: David Fulton Publishers

Katz, L. (2005) Foreword to Dowling, M., *Young Children's Personal, Social and Emotional Development*, London: Paul Chapman Publishing

Kotler, A., Wegerif, R. and LeVoi, M. (2001) 'Oracy and the educational achievement of pupils with English as an Additional Language: the impact of bringing "Talking Partners" into Bradford schools', *International Journal of Bilingual Education and Bilingualism*, 4:6, pp. 403–19

Kubuir Ross, E. *On Death and Dying*, New York: Macmillan.

Lapper, A. (2005) *My Life in My Hands*, London: Pocket Books

Lawrence, D. (1996) *Enhancing Self-Esteem in the Classroom*, London: Paul Chapman Publishing

Lawson, W. (1998) *Life Behind Glass: A Personal Account of Autism Spectrum Disorder*, Lismore, NSW: SCU Press

Levin, P. (1982) 'The cycle of development', *Transactional Analysis Journal*, 12:2, pp. 129–39

Lewis, S. (1998) 'Reading and writing within an oral/aural approach', in Gregory, S., Knight, P., McCracken, W., Powers, S. and Watson, L. (eds) *Issues in Deaf Education*, London: David Fulton Publishers

Lloyd, J., Lieven, E. and Arnold, P. (2001) Oral conversations between hearing-impaired children and their normally hearing peers and teachers', *First Language*, 21, pp. 83–107

MacConville, R. M. (1989) 'Service management for hearing impaired children', in Bowers, T. (ed.) *Managing Special Needs*, Milton Keynes: Open University Press

MacConville, R. M. (1991) 'A support services response to the 1988 Act', in Bowers, T. (ed.) *Schools, Services and Special Educational Needs: Management Issues in the Wake of LMS*, Cambridge: Perspective Press

MacConville, R. M. (2006a) 'Power to the pupils', *Children Now*, March, p. 23

MacConville, R. M. (2006b) 'Powerful voices', *Special Children*, February/March, p. 33–7

MacConville R. M. and Rae, T. (2006) *Teaching Peer Support for Caring and Co-operation: Talk Time*, Bristol: Lucky Duck Publishing

Maslow, A. H. (1968) *Towards a Psychology of Being*, New York: Van Nostrand.

Mason, M. L. (1998) *Guidelines for Teachers and Parents of Young People with a Visual Impairment Using Low Vision Aids (LVAs)*, Birmingham: University of Birmingham, School of Education

Measor, L. and Woods, P. (1984) *Changing Schools*, Milton Keynes: Open University Press

Mehrabian, A. (1972) *Nonverbal Communications*, Chicago, IL: Aldine Press

Mesbov, G. and Howley, M. (2003) *Accessing the Curriculum for Pupils with Autistic Spectrum Disorder: Using the TEACCH Programme to Help Inclusion*, London: David Fulton Publishers

Millar, S. (1994) *Understanding and Representing Space: Theory and Evidence from Studies with Blind and Sighted Children*, Oxford: Oneworld

Miller, O. and Ockelford, A. (2005) *Visual Needs*, London: Continuum

Moore, M., Beazley, S. and Maelzer, J. (1998) *Researching Disability Issues*, Buckingham: Open University Press

Moorehead, J. (2005) 'Is dyslexia just a myth?' *Guardian*, Education Section, 7 September

Murray, D. (1997) 'Autism and information technology: therapy with computers', in Powell, S. and Jordan, R. (eds) *Autism and Learning: A Guide to Good Practice*, London: David Fulton Publishers

NDCS (National Deaf Children's Society) (1999) *PATHS: The Way Towards Personal and Social Empowerment for Deaf Children*, London: National Deaf Children's Society

NDCS (National Deaf Children's Society) (2006) *'Has Anyone Thought to Include Me?' Fathers' Perceptions of Having a Deaf Child and the Services that Support Them*, London: National Deaf Children's Society

Newton, C., Taylor, G. and Wilson, D. (1996) 'Circles of Friends', *Educational Psychology in Practice*, January, pp. 41–8.

Nias, J. (1991) *Primary Teachers Talking: A Study of Teaching as Work*, London: Routledge

Nunes, T., Pretzlik, U. and Olsson, J. (2001) 'Deaf children's social relationships in mainstream schools', *Deafness and Education International*, 3:3, pp. 123–36

Ofsted (Office for Standards in Education) (1999) *Special Education 1994–98: A Review of Special Schools, Secure Units, Pupil Referral Units in England*, London: HMSO

O'Moore, M. (2000) 'Critical issues for teacher training to counter bullying and victimisation in Ireland', *Aggressive Behaviour*, 26:1, pp. 99–111

Ozonoff, S. and Miller, J., (1995) 'Teaching theory of mind: A new approach to Social skills training for individuals with autism'. *Journal of Autism and Developmental Disorders*, 25, pp. 415–33

Palincsar, A. S. and Brown, A. L. (1984) 'Reciprocal teaching of comprehension-fostering and comprehension-monitoring activities', *Cognition and Instruction*, 1:2, pp. 117–75

Palmer, S. (2006) *Toxic Childhood*, London: Orion Books

Pearpoint, J., Forest, M. and Snow, J. (1992) *The Inclusion Papers*, Cheshire: Inclusion Press

Peer, L. (2005) *Glue Ear*, London: David Fulton Publishers

Peer, L. and Reid, G. (2001) *Introduction to Dyslexia*, London: David Fulton Publishers

Pollock, J. and Walker, E. (1994) *Day to Day Dyslexia in the Classroom*, London: Routledge

Powell, S. (2000) *Helping Children with Autism to Learn*, London: David Fulton Publishers

Powers, S. (1999) 'Deaf and hearing impaired pupils learning mainly via aided hearing', in Watson, L., Gregory, S. and Powers, S. (eds) *Deaf and Hearing Impaired Pupils in Mainstream Schools*, London: David Fulton Publishers

Quentin, J. (2003) 'An investigation into the playground experiences of pupils with special educational needs', in MacConville R. M. (ed.) *Inclusion: A Celebration of Good Practice in Ealing*, London: London Borough of Ealing

Quinn, P. (1998) *Understanding Disability: A Life Span Approach*, London: Sage Publications

Reid, G. (2005) *Dyslexia*, London: Continuum

RIBA (Royal Institute of British Architects) (1981) *Lighting and Acoustic Criteria for the Visually Handicapped and Hearing Impaired in Schools*, London: HMSO

Riddick, B. (1996) *Living with Dyslexia: The Social and Emotional Consequences of Specific Learning Difficulties*, London: Routledge

Rose, R. and Shevlin, M. (2004) 'Encouraging voices: listening to young people who have been marginalised', *Support for Learning*, 19:4 pp. 155–61

Ross, M. (1991) *Hearing Impaired Children in the Mainstream*, Parkton, MD: York Press

Sainsbury, C. (2000) *Martian in the Playground*, Bristol: Lucky Duck Publishing

Scott, R. (2003) 'A counsellor's perspective on dyslexia', in Thomson, M. (ed.) *Dyslexia Included*, London: David Fulton Publishers

Sebba, J., Byers, R. and Rose, R. (1993) *Redefining the Whole Curriculum*, London: David Fulton Publishers

Seligiman, M. E. P. (2002) *Authentic Happiness*, London: Nicholas Brealey Publishing

Sharp, P. (2001) *Nurturing Emotional Literacy*, London: David Fulton Publishers

Sinclair, J. (1989) 'Bridging the gaps: an inside-out view of autism', from his website: http://web.syr.edu/~jsincla/

Social Market Foundation (2006) 'Curriculum revamp is called for', *Emotional Literacy Update*, 28

Stanovitch, K. E. (1994) 'Annotation: does dyslexia exist?', *Journal of Child Psychology and Psychiatry*, 5:4, pp. 579–95

Stinson, M. S., Whitmore, K. and Kluwin, T. N. (1996) Self-perceptions of social relationships in hearing impaired adolescents', *Journal of Educational Psychology*, 88:1, pp. 132–43

Sullivan, H. S. (1953) *The Interpersonal Theory of Psychiatry*, New York: Norton

Thomas, G., Walker, D. and Webb, J. (1998) *The Making of the Inclusive School*, London: Routledge

Thomas, N. and O'Kane, C. (1998) 'The ethics of participatory research with children', *Children and Society*, 12, pp. 336–48

Thompson, M., O'Neill Grace, C. with Cohen, L. J. (2001) *Best Friends, Worst Enemies: Children's Friendships, Popularity and Social Cruelty*, London: Penguin/Michael Joseph

Tobin, M. J. (1998) 'Is blindness a handicap?', *British Journal of Special Education*, 25:3, pp. 107–13

Trevarthen, C. (1992) 'An infant's motives for thinking and speaking', in Wold, A. H. (ed.) *The Dialogical Alternative*, Oxford: Oxford University Press

Tunmer, W. E. and Chapman, J. (1996) 'A developmental model of dyslexia', *Dyslexia*, 2:3, pp. 179–89

Tyrell, J. (2002) *Peer Mediation: A Process for Primary Schools*, London: Souvenir Press

Vygotsky, L. (1978) *Mind in Society: The Development of Higher Psychological Processes*, Cambridge, MA: Harvard University Press

Warren, D. H. (1994) *Blindness and Children: An Individual Differences Approach*, Cambridge: Cambridge University Press

Weinbren, H. and Gill, P. (1998) 'Narratives of childhood epilepsy: have I got epilepsy or has it got me?', in Greenhalgh, T. and Hurwitz, B. (eds) *Narrative Based Medicine: Dialogue and Discourse in Clinical Practice*, London: BMJ Books

Welding, J. (1996) 'In-class support: a successful way of meeting individual need?', *Support for Learning*, 11:3, pp. 113–17

Whitaker, P. (2001) *Challenging Behaviour and Autism: Making Sense – Making Progress*, London: National Autistic Society

Whitaker, P., Barrett, J., Potter, M. and Thompson, G. (1998) 'Children with autism and peer group support: using Circle of Friends', *British Journal of Special Education*, 25:2, pp. 60–4

Whizz Kids (2003) *Summary Report on the Midlands 'Break Down Barriers' Conference on Representations of Disabled People on TV, 'Disability on the Box'*, 21 November 2003, London: Whizz Kids

Wing, L. (1981) 'Asperger's syndrome: a clinical account', *Psychological Medicine*, 11, pp. 115–30

YouGov (2003) *Opinion Poll for the Charity Changing Faces*, London: Changing Faces